A Geographia Guide

D0505249

Scottish Lowlands

Edinburgh, the Clyde, and Border Country

INCLUDING

- EDINBURGH CASTLE
- DUNBAR
- COLDSTREAM
- DALKEITH
- GLASGOW
- THE CLYDE
- BLANTYRE
- LANARK
- AYR
- KILMARNOCK
- NEWTON STEWART
- KIRKCUDBRIGHT
- DUMFRIES
- ABBOTSFORD
- SELKIRK
- GRETNA GREEN

Geographia Ltd
63 Fleet Street
London, E.C.4

Guide to Scottish Lowlands
© Geographia Ltd.,
63 Fleet Street,
London, E.C.4

_____

Compiled and published by
Geographia Ltd.

_____

Text: H. O. Wade

_____

Photographic illustrations
British Tourist Authority
Line Drawings: G. Cowan, W. Balmain

_____

Series Editor: J. T. Wright

_____

Made and printed in Great Britain by
The Anchor Press Ltd.,
Tiptree, Essex

Contents

Illustrations

Section 1 Introduction

To most people Southern Scotland is almost synonymous with the Border country, the land of centuries of border raid and counter raid; of famous Border towns, Selkirk, Melrose, Jedburgh and others; of Border abbeys, Melrose and Jedburgh; of countless Border peles and castles. Many of them are still in existence and some are still occupied. This is a land that has been conditioned very largely by those centuries of Border warfare and even today, an aura of those tragic times pervades the immediate surroundings of many of the Border towns but more particularly the peles and castles of those far-off days.

Act of Union

Since peace came to this beautiful land on the Union of the Crowns of Scotland and England in 1603, more than three and a half centuries ago, Southern Scotland has made tremendous strides forward and has transformed the living conditions of the kindly Scottish people, but, happily for the visitor, great areas of the countryside remain much as they always have been. Along the southern border with England, where Sir Walter Scott roamed as a boy, the hills, the valleys,

St. Mary s Loch

the rivers and burns look more or less as they were. From the green valleys to the heather-topped hills, from the rugged eastern coast to the immense expanse of the Solway, to the varied coastline of the west; from the rich plains of Ayrshire, where Robert Burns was born, to the glorious broken country of Galloway and the soft heather-covered slopes of the Lammermuirs; from the Forest of Trool to the ancient Ettrick Forest, from the lovely lochs of the west and centre to the unsurpassed Valley of the Tweed, Southern Scotland can offer as great a variety of scenery as any other part of these islands.

Nationalism

The Scots, both men and women, are perhaps the most nationalistic of the peoples of the British Isles. A Scot is always a Scot and not just British as most English people are content to be. Since 1603 they have had no King of their own, since 1707 no separate parliament; their independence was virtually taken from them by the historic agreement of the Act of Union. Yet they have never lost their sense of nationhood, of being Scots first and last. This fact should be kept in mind when meeting Scots and exploring their country. It will help you to understand the people, their works and accomplishments.

Eminent Citizens

This is a land that, in spite of its very warlike and tragic history, in spite of it being a land that is not rich agriculturally overall, it has produced great numbers of eminent citizens, among whom especially have been soldiers, engineers and colonial administrators. Sir Walter Scott was the most famous of Scottish writers and Robert Burns the most loved and best remembered of the poets. Scotland, throughout its history a poor land, has taken a full part in the cultural, industrial and agricultural progress of these islands and played a very big part indeed in the colonisation of the British Empire during the seventeenth, eighteenth and nineteenth centuries. Canada in particular owes much to the explorers and early colonists from Scotland.

Industry and Beauty

The area covered by this guide extends from the border with England to the Edinburgh—Glasgow motorway across the narrow neck of Scotland. Between the two great cities of Edinburgh and Glasgow, and for a few miles south, there is a large industrial conurbation reaching right across the width of the country; this we shall deal with separately. Southwards from this admittedly ugly but necessary sprawl, and apart from a few partly industrial towns, Southern Scotland is all wide open country with good roads, good hotels and all the amenities the modern visitor needs. Perhaps the greatest attraction is the comparatively uncrowded state of the roads, and this particularly applies to that broad and very beautiful sweep of country known as Galloway. It is a land of twisting lanes and tiny hidden coves on a delightful yet very uncrowded sea-shore. This lovely piece of country is well served by first-class roads and will probably attract the caravanner and camper more than others.

New Names

Although new administrative boundaries became operative from May 1975, the traditional county names are used throughout this Guide. Current boundaries and names may be seen on the map inside the back cover.

Motoring

As a motorist you are probably on holiday and looking for peace and quiet; or you may prefer fast roads and good hotels. Southern Scotland can please both types. There are, in all, some twenty-four towns with reasonable to good hotels and all are connected by first-class roads. Many of them are close to some of the finest scenery and the connecting roads all pass through some of the loveliest country in the area covered. The Tweed Valley road from Berwick-on-Tweed to Kelso, Galashiels, Peebles and Moffat is an outstanding example. Another is the secondary but very good road from Moffat to Tweedsmuir, St. Mary's Loch and Selkirk. A third example, among many, is the road from Ayr to Castle Douglas by Loch Doon.

Byways

For the motorist looking for quiet roads, and possibly suitable sites for his caravan, there are many secluded spots and roads where little traffic will be encountered, for example, the little by-roads close to the Border hills east of the A68, the Lammermuir Hills south-east of Edinburgh, the by-roads north-west of Hawick around the Ettrick Forest to Loch Long and Tweedsmuir; the Lowther Hills west of Moffat and the Glentrool Forest north of which is the Carrick Forest. All these places and many more offer the best scenery and the quietest roads; Galloway, however, is probably the area with the greatest choice and has coastal scenery that is difficult to beat. South of the main road from Dumfries to Stranraer lies much of the finest coast scenery with plenty of places for caravanning, few crowds and quiet roads.

Walking

For the keen walker Southern Scotland, with its immense areas of largely uninhabited hills and valleys, its glorious woodlands and beautiful lochs, offers an almost unmatched variety of countryside.

For The Experienced

The Glentrool Forest, and the area of Loch Trool and Loch Dee in west Kirkcudbrightshire, are among the most beautiful. Northwards from Loch Trool and Loch Dee for about 15 miles there is a virtually uninhabited stretch of country thickly dotted with lochs, burns and crags. There are many hills that top the 2,000-foot mark and many more over 1,500 feet. This is a stretch of very wild and broken country and should be treated with care and walked only by the fully experienced walker. For the professional it is, however, magnificent.

Herring Road

South-east of Edinburgh there is an area of softly rolling heather-clad hills, the Lammermuir Hills. These are ideal for the less experienced walker and allow plenty of exercise with map and compass. There are a number of old green tracks which cross these hills. The most important was the Herring Road along which the fisher-wives from Dunbar carried their baskets of fresh herring to the markets farther south. This track, and others, cannot be easily followed today but make a first-class objective and adds great interest to any walk.

Lowther Hills

Most of Selkirkshire and the southern parts of Peebleshire have some fine and varied walking country. The Lowther Hills in the south of Lanarkshire and the north of Dumfriesshire also make for first-class hill walking with plenty of 2,000-foot hills to climb. Again this is fairly wild country and the amateur should be very careful.

The Coasts

Both the east and west coasts are excellent and easier walking than the hills; with coastal scenery, in places of a very high order, and with the added attraction of never being far from roads and towns or villages, they should attract more and more walkers.

Easy Ground

Galloway, that verdant district which lies between Dumfries and Stranraer and extends southwards to the much broken coast, is an ideal walking ground for the less vigorous. The scenery is tremendously varied and the coastal scenery magnificent. The walking routes can be as short or as long as the individual requires and the coastal walks are truly unmatched.

Tweed Valley

The Border country, Roxburghshire and Berwickshire, also afford some grand walking and steep climbing, while the many footpaths along the Tweed Valley will give untold pleasure to those who prefer the green and pleasant valleys to the open moorland and the hills.

Be Prepared

For the amateur walker a few hints may be helpful. Remember that in the hills exposure can be suffered even in the summer time. This is a dangerous state that creeps over one without one's knowledge. Always walk warmly clad with a spare and warm jersey in the rucksack. Wear trousers, not shorts, and always carry waterproofs, including trousers. Carry food and a hot drink or a spirit stove. Water is almost always to be found. Learn to read a map and compass and never go out on the moorlands and hills without them—detailed Ordnance Survey map is the best. Always plan your walk and always leave word as to where you intend going. If you do get lost, and it is very easy in the fog, then rescuers will know where to look. Remember that the weather can change very quickly in the hills; take the necessary precautions and learn to know the job of walking. Then you will get the best out of it and really enjoy the hills and moors.

Geology
by Dr. D. A. Robson

Some four hundred million years ago Scotland was the scene of violent and prolonged earth movements. These movements were most intense in the extreme north, where layers of rock were folded and pushed across one another, providing the foundation for the mountainous region of the Central, Western and North-Western Highlands. South of the Highlands, the earth movements were less severe and the strata were compressed, concertina fashion, into long folds trending south-west to north-east. Today, these folded strata, described collectively as the Lower Palaeozoic rocks, form the great hill barrier known as the Southern Uplands, which separates the low-lying Edinburgh and Glasgow industrial belt from the Border country. The rocks themselves are very well exposed along the north-east coast in the neighbourhood of St. Abb's Head, and along the south-west coast from the Mull of Galloway to the Solway.

Pentland Hills

Following upon this great period of earth movement, volcanic activity took place on a wide scale. In the south, the Cheviot Hills were formed, while to the north extensive eruptions created the great ridges of the Ochil and Sidlaw Hills. In the neighbourhood of what is now Edinburgh, volcanoes poured out lava flows which today form the Pentland Hills. Furthermore, there were great intrusions of granite —molten rock which was forced vertically up into the earth's crust— notably in the centre of the Cheviot lavas, and at Criffel and elsewhere in south-west Scotland. All this subterranean activity, which invariably accompanies and succeeds prolonged periods of earth movement, occurred in Old Red Sandstone times, about 350 million years ago.

Volcanic Activity

While this volcanic activity was in progress, rivers were flowing south from the newly created Highlands. They poured their debris of boulders, pebbles and sand across the great undulating plain which stretched as far as the Cheviots, for the Southern Uplands region did not yet form such a distinct barrier as it does today. (The situation was not unlike that in northern India at the present day, where rivers emerging from the Himalayas spread broken rubble from the high mountains across the Indian plain.)

Stone for Building

In course of time, the débris from the Highlands became indurated to form the rocks of the Old Red Sandstone age. At Jedburgh, and especially at Sickar Point on the north-east coast, these sandstones can be seen lying across the tilted and worn-down edges of the Lower Palaeozoic rocks. In the Cheviot country they can be shown to overlie and to be overlain by the individual lava flows. Much of the rock outcropping across the Scottish Border country belongs to this Old Red succession; it forms the cliffs beside the Jed Water, over-looking the Edinburgh road; it has been quarried extensively for building (it provided the stone for the famous Border Abbeys) and it readily breaks down to form the characteristic red soil of the district.

Coal Seams

During the succeeding geological period, that of the Carboniferous, deposits derived from the Highlands continued to be laid down across the centre of Scotland; these deposits formed sandstones and shales. In addition marine conditions prevailed in the Edinburgh to Glasgow area and limestones were formed. At other times there was thick vegetation which in due time was transformed into coal-seams.

During the Carboniferous period, volcanic activity also took place again, though on a more reduced scale than hitherto. The rocky cliffs beneath Edinburgh Castle, the great hump of Arthur's Seat and nearby Calton Hill, together with the Campsie Fells and Kilpatrick Hills of Glasgow, all witness to this renewed activity. Volcanoes also developed across the Border country—their stumps are still there forming the craggy hills of which the Eildons and Rubers Law are the most noteworthy. These events occurred about 350 million years ago.

Southern Upland Fault

Later formations of rock were almost certainly laid down over those which have just been described, but of their existence no trace now remains. Further earth-movements also occurred, of which the most important were those producing the Southern Uplands fault; this is the fracture which, cutting across the whole of Scotland, uplifted the barrier of the Southern Uplands to its present position.

Glacial Epoch

The most recent geological event was that of the Ice Age, when the whole countryside was buried beneath the glaciers which pushed south from the Highlands. The ice sharpened the crags of Edinburgh and the volcanic stumps of the Border country, but cut through the neighbouring soft deposits. As the glaciers melted, valleys were partially infilled with the debris which the ice had accumulated in its southerly course. Therefore, today both the uplands and the lowlands of the region bears the imprint of the glacial epoch which lasted for a million years and which ended a mere 10,000 years ago.

Wildlife
by W. Balmain

The visitor to Southern Scotland will quickly become aware that the contrast within this area is immense. To the west is a magnificent range of mountains, truly Scottish in every sense of the word; there are forests, rich farmlands, moorland, lochs, burns and rivers, and both in the west and east rugged coastlines, sand dunes, pebble beaches, saltings and tiny bays. A variety of country indeed and such variety affords in turn a rich habitat for numerous species of wild life.

Golden Eagle

Perhaps the greatest symbol of Scottish wild life, the Golden Eagle, has now returned again to its old haunts in the Glen Trool Forest area. On the high grounds across the country Red and Black Grouse can be seen, and the Curlew, Green and Golden Plovers send their liquid notes across heather and heath. The Buzzard, Merlin and Kestrel search for prey on the lonely moors, and, occasionally, that prince among birds, the Peregrine Falcon, stoops down from the sky. In forest and on crags the Raven sends a deep croak down to us as if to protest at our intrusion into the lonely territory he loves.

Hooded Crow

Beginning at Wigtown in the west and describing a rough "up and across" arc across country, we enter a surprisingly narrow 15 to 20 mile band which marks the range of the Hooded Crows of the North and Carrion Crow. Within this band we find many intermediate varieties. Bird life is abundant everywhere and reports of counting 128 species in Galloway alone can be taken as feasible.

Sea-birds

On the coasts many sea-birds can be seen, for there are breeding sites both on the coast and offshore on tiny islands. On the east coast in Firth of Forth, Dunlin and Redshank wade, Terns breed on the islands and thousands of Duck can be seen in season. St Abbs Head affords high cliffs for breeding birds. On the other side of Southern Scotland on the west coast we find the same sanctuary. Saltmarsh and mud-flats attract flocks of Pink-footed and Greylag Geese. The great cliffs of the Mull of Galloway induce Fulmar, Guillemot, Shags, Kittiwake, Greater and Lesser Black Backed and Herring Gulls to nest. Oystercatchers grace all coastal areas.

Basking Shark

In the warm waters of Luce Bay one may even see the Basking Shark offshore in the tidal rips of the Mull. Whooper Swans fly in during winter months; during winter time too Fieldfares and Redwings arrive by the thousand.

Giant Grouse

In Kirroughtree Forest Golden and Amerherst Pheasants light up the dark forests with their brilliant plumage, and passing through Glenluce the Giant Grouse or Capercaille has been seen. Glen Trool is unique as the most "highland" district south of the highlands themselves and here the mighty roar of feral Red Deer can be heard and the beasts themselves are sometimes seen in small herds running completely wild and free. Fallow Deer wander from deer parks and establish themselves in the wild occasionally. That "Bambi" amongst deer, the Roe, can be found right across the country wherever there is a forest, wood, or some cover where they may lie up during daylight hours.

Red Squirrel

Foxes inhabit high and low ground and a few Otters still linger near the quiet rivers and streams. Red squirrels are found in low-lying woodland and forest areas.

Blue Mountain Hare

On the Scottish side of the Cheviots wild goats sometimes can be seen against the skyline, and on the hills above Glen Trool, a herd with long sweeping horns may be viewed by the patient and quiet wanderer. On most of the high grounds Blue Mountain Hares and Stoats in Ermine run but are not easily seen when winter spreads her white mantle across the hills.

Gannets

From the lonely outpost islands of Ailsa Craig off the west coast to Bass Rock off the east coast—both home to thousands of Gannets— wild life flourishes throughout Southern Scotland in numbers that give surprised delight to the traveller.

How to Get There

By Train: There are two main lines into Southern Scotland from England, the old North Eastern and North British via Newcastle-upon-Tyne and Berwick-on-Tweed to Edinburgh, and the old London and North Western and Caledonian via Carlisle to Glasgow. Both supply a fast and frequent service. The Waverley line, the North British, connecting with the Midland from St. Pancras, was closed in the early part of 1969, but plans are afoot to reopen it as a private company. There are first-rate services from the north of Scotland to Edinburgh and from the west coast to Glasgow with an hourly service connecting the two cities.

By Road: There are five main roads into Southern Scotland from England, the Great North Road or A1 via Berwick-on-Tweed, the A68 from Newcastle-upon-Tyne over Carter Bar to Jedburgh, the A7 from Carlisle to Hawick along the Teviot Water, the A74 from Carlisle to Glasgow over Beattock, and the A75 from Carlisle through Gretna to Annan and Dumfries. These are all good roads and all have their attractive and scenic points. The finest entrance into Southern Scotland, if one wants to taste in full the flavour of the Border, is via the North Tyne and Langholm. Go through Hexham, Bellingham, Kielder, Deadwater, turn right about three miles before Newcastleton and through Hermitage, with the historical castle of ill-repute, to Langholm, the most Border-like of all the Border towns.

By Bus and Coach: There is a first-class bus and coach service into most places in Southern Scotland by all five of the main roads mentioned above. From Newcastle-upon-Tyne, Berwick-on-Tweed, Carlisle or Dumfries almost any town in the area dealt with may be reached quickly and comfortably.

By Air: Southern Scotland is particularly lucky in having three large airports. Prestwick, on the south-west coast near Ayr, is the transatlantic air terminus, and, being almost entirely fog-free, handles most of the Atlantic services. Glasgow Airport at Abbotsinch, just west of the City in Renfrewshire, is the busiest aviation centre in Scotland. It is the terminal of the London–Glasgow route, and provides services to Aberdeen, the Highlands and Islands, most important centres in the United Kingdom, and Continental flights to such widely scattered places as Copenhagen, Ostend, Amsterdam, Paris and Palma. Turnhouse Airport, about six miles west of Edinburgh, operates services by British European Airways, Aer Lingus (International) Air Lines, British United Airways, B.K.S. Air Transport Ltd. and British Midland Airways. London, Aberdeen and Inverness, which has connections for further north, Glasgow, Manchester and Birmingham, are some of the places served by regular flights.

Section 2   Edinburgh and the Eastern Borders

EDINBURGH

Population: 467,986.
Early Closing Day: Tuesday, Wednesday and Saturday. Varies throughout the City.
Tourist Information Centre: 23, Ravelston Terrace
Museums and Art Galleries: Canongate Tolbooth; Huntley House, Canongate; Lauriston Castle, Davidsons Mains; Lady Stair's House (housing a Sir Walter Scott and Robert Burns Museum); Museum of Childhood, Hyndford's Close; National Gallery of Scotland; National Museum of Antiquities of Scotland; The Royal Scottish Museum; Scottish National Portrait Gallery; Scottish United Services Museum.

EDINBURGH IS NOT ONLY THE capital of Scotland but in many ways the most impressive and most exciting city in the British Isles. The best known and probably the busiest street is Princes Street, lined with handsome buildings along the north side while the south side is completely taken up with the Princes Street Gardens, and beautiful gardens they are, the Scott Monument and the Castle on its rugged hill-top with the 800 feet of Arthur's Seat tending to dominate the whole scene. It is this magnificent picture that creates such a vivid and lasting impression of Edinburgh, the capital of a strong and virile nation with a patriotism unscathed by the many tragic centuries.

Volcanic Plug

It is not known just when Edinburgh started life but it is safe to assume that, when the Romans first stood on Soutra Summit and looked down on the broad estuary of the Forth, Edinburgh had begun life with a few very primitive dwellings on the volcanic plug which later became the centre of the City and the site of Edinburgh Castle. Reliable records of the Castle exist from the eleventh century, when King Malcolm III resided there. By the sixteenth century Edinburgh was still housed on the rock and by the seventeenth century had spread only to the Palace of Holyrood House. It was in 1767 that

Parliament, in London, for the Edinburgh Parliament died in 1707,
approved a plan for the extension of Edinburgh northwards across the
Nor'Loch. The plan was designed by James Craig, a 23-year-old
architect: It was promptly and almost entirely put into effect with the
result we see today, Queen Street, George Street, and Princes Street
named after King George, his Queen and the Prince of Wales.

The Royal Mile

The Royal Mile, which comprises the Esplanade, Castle Hill,
Lawnmarket, Parliament Square, High Street and Canongate, runs
from the Castle to the Palace of Holyrood House and was, during the
Middle Ages, the centre of Edinburgh life. Along this magnificent
promenade, with numerous old and historic buildings, some dating
back to the seventeenth century, the council have done a great work
in restoration and rejuvenation so that it is now worthy of the great
city of which it was once the most important thoroughfare.

Castle Rock

There are so many interesting places, so many beautiful scenes, so
many things worthy of note that we must be content here with an outline of the most notable; so let us start where Edinburgh itself started,
on the Castle Rock. This volcanic plug—some authorities believe it is
an extinct volcano—is 443 feet above sea-level and 270 feet above
West Princes Street Gardens, and from it may be had some remarkable
views of Edinburgh.

EDINBURGH CASTLE

The Castle of Edinburgh sits four-square atop the Castle Hill, its
battlements overlooking the Esplanade, once the scene of
executions, but today more pleasantly associated with the famous
Military Tattoos which are such a feature of the world-famous
Edinburgh Festival which takes place at the end of August.

Although the site always held a fortress or defensive structure, it
was first really known as such in the seventh century in the reign
of King Edwin of Northumbria: his kingdom then stretched from the
Channel coast of Wessex up to the Firth of Forth. Indeed, 'Scotia's
darling seat' as Burns called it, derived its name from that
king—being first called 'Edwin's burgh'.

A more detailed history of the Castle appears in the eleventh
century, long after Edwin's death and the breaking-up of the former
Saxon kingdoms. By that time Scotland was a larger, and separate,
kingdom ruled by Malcolm III (Canmore), son of the murdered
Duncan I, the victim of Macbeth. His queen was the very religious

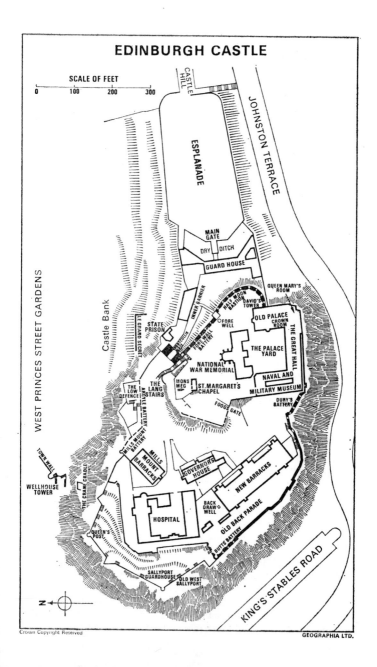

Margaret, sister of the Atheling, heir to the Saxon royal House of Cerdic, who had been displaced by William the Conqueror.

St. Margaret's Chapel

After her death, the queen became known as 'Saint Margaret' and the chapel she built, still called St. Margaret's Chapel, is all that remains of the Castle in which she lived. Although it was not until the sixteenth century that Edinburgh became the capital of Scotland, the castle in its various stages of development was often used as a royal residence.

The Esplanade, from which the Castle is best approached, dates in its present form from the eighteenth century, and the various buildings which became part of the Castle were mostly fitted-in with the existing general fortifications, according to need and the space available.

Palace Yard

The buildings set in the Palace Yard comprise the 'Citadel' or core of the Castle. Here, around what used to be 'The Close' stands the Palace, or King's Lodging, the Great Hall, and the Officers' Quarters, dating from the reign of Queen Anne. In front of these buildings stands the National War Memorial of Scotland, the work of Sir Robert Lorimer: it was unveiled by the Prince of Wales (afterwards the Duke of Windsor), in 1927. It has a fine Gallery of Honour, handsome bays, and finely carved figures. In the archway is a shrine protected by attractively designed gates. In the interior are carved the names of the great Scottish regiments, whether raised at home or overseas.

'Mons Meg'

To the east of the Palace is Half Moon Bastion, or gun platform behind which were uncovered the ruins of King David I's Tower. Behind St. Margaret's Chapel is the famous giant gun made at Mons in 1486. This is 'Mons Meg' which featured in so many of the earlier Scottish wars. Though it was removed to the Tower of London in 1754, George IV, influenced by Sir Walter Scott who was a favourite with him, had the gun restored to the Castle.

Mary Queen of Scots

The Royal Apartments, although not very regal, are interesting. They contain historic portraits, mementoes and documents; a special attraction is Queen Mary's bedroom. This was the birthplace, in June 1566, of James VI of Scotland and I of England: Mary Queen of Scots, his mother, had taken refuge there with her estranged husband Darnley, when they were apparently reconciled. She stayed in the Royal Apartments again before her strange marriage to the Earl of Bothwell which took place in Holyrood Palace at the eastern end of Canongate. Queen Mary never returned here, although it was from these apartments that Morton claimed to have found the notorious Casket of letters which implicated her in Bothwell's crimes.

Crown Room

In the Crown Room repose the Scottish Regalia, or 'Honours of Scotland' as they are called. They consist of the crown, sceptre, sword of state, and other royal jewels which, unlike their English counterparts, were successfully hidden from Cromwell's men who wished to destroy all such symbols, and to make more practical use of the wealth they represented.

The Batteries

Where the gun 'Mons Meg' stands, and east of Queen Margaret's Chapel, are the famous 'Lang Stairs', while to the west of the ground at this level, below the Citadel, are The Governor's House, the New Barracks, and the Hospital etc., all mainly of eighteenth century character, although part of the hospital is modern. Around the walls are the Butts Battery, the Mills Mount Battery and the Argyle Battery which overlooks West Princes Street. The road down from the Argyle Battery passes under Portcullis Gate with its overhead chamber, via the inner barrier and out to the Esplanade.

Fortunes of War

Most of the sixteenth and seventeenth century history of the Castle concerns the changing fortunes of war, with long sieges, distinguished prisoners such as Montrose and later his great rival the Earl of Argyll. Bonnie Prince Charlie failed to capture the castle, and thereafter it remained mainly a prison for French soldiers from the Napoleonic wars.

Popular Venue

Today it is a garrison still, an historic place with a romantic past, and a popular venue for visitors, both for itself and for the lively Military Tattoos already mentioned.

Camera Obscura

The nearby Outlook Tower houses an exhibition of Scottish life through the centuries and a camera obscura, with the aid of which some quite amazing views of Edinburgh and her immediate surroundings can be seen on the white concave table-top. Just off Lawnmarket is a fine tall building called Gladstone's Land. This is the last of the seventeenth-century buildings left in Edinburgh. It has an outside stair, crow-stepped gables and painted ceilings, and is owned by the National Trust for Scotland.

Holyrood House

The Palace of Holyrood House is now the official residence of the Queen when visiting Edinburgh and, during the General Assembly of the Church of Scotland, of the Queen's representative, the Lord High

Copyright: *GEOGRAPHIA LTD.*   Crown Copyright Reserved.

Commissioner. In 1128 King David I founded the Abbey of Holyrood, and early in the sixteenth century, when James IV made Edinburgh the capital of Scotland, he took the Abbey guest-house for his palace. His extravagant plans for rebuilding were never completed. Most of what the visitor sees today was the work of Charles II, who began rebuilding in 1671. Among the most interesting things to be seen are 111 portraits of Scottish Kings. The tapestries and furnishings in the State apartments and the Throne room are rare and very beautiful. Of the Abbey itself, founded in 1128, the greater part of the thirteenth-century stone-vaulted nave is still there, while of the twelfth century, the original work, only a rebuilt east processional doorway and some foundations remain. To lovers of the old and beautiful this can be a very rewarding visit.

The High Kirk

St. Giles's Cathedral, noted as the High Kirk of Edinburgh and the very heart of Scotland, is the latest in a line of churches that have occupied this site, alongside the Royal Mile. The original St. Giles's was a Norman building of 1120. Of this only the four octagonal pillars under the Tower, on which is the Crown of St. Giles, remain. This is a truly fascinating old church with many interesting and historical remains. The Chapel of the Most Ancient and Most Noble Order of the Thistle is not only the loveliest part of the Cathedral but is the most delightful and ornate building erected in Scotland since the Middle Ages. There are a great many chapels reviving memories of various periods of Scotland's history as well as many of her famous families. By the middle of the sixteenth century the last vestige of the Roman Church had disappeared, and many of the most ornate trappings and furnishings had been destroyed.

Mercat Cross

Near the east door of St. Giles's Cathedral is the Mercat Cross. Mercat crosses, in all parts of the country, usually mark the spot where markets were held, business transacted and, sometimes, executions carried out; Royal proclamations were always made from the Mercat Cross. Behind the Cathedral is Parliament House, where the Scots parliament met until 1707 and the final Union of Scotland and England. It is now the home of Scotland's supreme courts, both civil and criminal. By the Act of Union in 1707 the Scottish people have always retained their own law courts and a great many of their own laws. In Parliament Hall is a particularly fine hammer-beam roof, a number of portraits and a monument to Sir Walter Scott, who was born in Edinburgh in 1771.

Tron Kirk

The Tron Kirk, at the crossing of High Street and the North and South Bridges, is a very beautiful relic of 1637. Nearly all the churches built during the seventeenth and eighteenth centuries were very severe in outline and with a minimum of ornament, plain churches from which the Reformed minister could preach. Tron, among a very few others, is a shining example of revived Gothic. And a very moving and beautiful little church it is. The Tron was a weighing beam for checking merchants' weights; if at fault the merchants were nailed by their ears to the Tron, which stood outside the church. A little farther on is Carrubber's Close leading to Old St. Paul's Episcopal Church, which came into being as a result of the disestablishment of the Anglican or Episcopal Church for its loyalty to the Jacobite cause and its refusal to accept William of Orange as King. For 200 years the congregation worshipped in a wool store on the site where the church was built in 1883. Scots, more than most peoples, have been most unwilling to change their beliefs to order.

John Knox

Still in the High Street is John Knox's house. John Knox was one of the greatest of the Reformers of the Scottish Church and the most outspoken of them all. He probably lived in this house from 1561 to 1572 when, for at least part of this time, he was minister of St. Giles. The house was built in 1490 and is the sole remaining house with the timber galleries, once so common.

The Tolbooth

A little farther on is Canongate, named after the Canons of Holyrood Abbey. It was the aristocratic quarter of old Edinburgh and some of the large houses have been renovated, and a few house museums. Still in Canongate is Huntly House, a half-timbered house of 1517. Opposite is the Tolbooth. This is a particularly Scottish building as are most of the Scottish Town Houses or Tolbooths, and was built in 1592 as the Town House of the old Burgh of Canongate; it has been used as a jail. The Scottish Town House or Tolbooth is roughly equivalent to the English Town Hall. A little farther along Canongate is the Parish Church of the one-time Burgh of Canongate, and at the end of this famous street is one of the most picturesque spots in Edinburgh, White Horse Close, that was, during the coaching era, the terminus of the London Mail and passenger service.

University

In Chambers Street, which is a turning off South Bridge, are several colleges, the Edinburgh University Theatre and Conference Hall, while in South Bridge itself is the chief University building, the Old College. The University was founded in 1582 and the Old College was erected in 1789 to 1834. In nearby Forrest Road is the Kirk of Greyfriars, where the National Covenant was signed in 1638. Here also is the memorial to the Covenanters.

Australian Rival

To many people Princes Street and the extremely beautiful gardens will prove the most alluring feature of Edinburgh. The complete picture, Princes Street, the Gardens, the Castle and the Scott monument are incomparable, except only with St. Kilda's Avenue in Melbourne, Australia. The shops are in keeping with the general appearance and women will find Edinburgh a most pleasant shopping centre and a popular place for a day's sightseeing.

Parks and Gardens

Of course there is another side to Edinburgh. Industry has its place and the usual signs of industry are not always pleasant and often unsightly; but there is sufficient of this noble City to explore without taking in the industrial areas, which areas are largely spread along the nine miles frontage to the Firth of Forth. The parks and gardens of Edinburgh are, in the right season, exceptionally fine and occupy a greater percentage of the City's area than almost any other town or city in the country. The chief parks and gardens are Princes Street, The Inch, Harrison, Inverleith, Victoria and Saughton; the latter has nine types of garden—rose, heath, iris, flower, bulb, shrub, herbaceous, sunk or Italian—and a so-called Blind Garden, where the special fragrance of the flowers can be enjoyed by the blind. Edinburgh must be one of the very few places which, within the City boundaries, has a hill not far short of 1,000 feet with three lochs and a trout stream, for the Water of Leith flows right through the City centre from south to north, finally reaching the sea at the Port of Leith. For children and lovers of animals there is the Edinburgh Zoo on the sunny slopes of Corstorphine Hill. In addition the Royal Botanic Gardens are an attraction to thousands.

Sporting Activities

For the sportsman or woman Edinburgh offers untold opportunities to participate or just to watch others. Golf was first played in Edinburgh in 1457 and must be accounted Scotland's own game. Edinburgh has 22 golf courses. Bowling is the other sport in which Edinburgh takes a prominent part, with 53 Corporation greens and 50 private clubs. Tennis, rugby, hockey, football, yachting, horse-riding, skiing and almost every known sport or recreation is well represented here.

International Festival

Little needs to be said about the cultural and artistic side of the life of Edinburgh. A Civic Theatre, the well-known International Festival, which now includes a Film Festival, a host of Museums, Art Galleries and other centres of cultural activity make Edinburgh a real capital of artistic and cultural life in Scotland. As a conference city Edinburgh is achieving a new fame, for she is rich in suitable halls of different seating capacity and very rich in all the things visitors like to see; in addition the atmosphere of Edinburgh is more restful than that of many other cities, while the transport facilities, to and from, are first rate.

Industrial Activities

From the foregoing it will be deduced that industry does not play the greatest part of life in Edinburgh, in fact only 25 per cent of the working population are employed in industry. Social services and administration take the lion's share. The main industrial activity is taken up with food, drink, tobacco, engineering, electrical goods, paper, printing and publishing. Printing was first established in 1507 and in 1768 the *Encyclopaedia Britannica* came to life in Edinburgh. Since that day this city has been one of the publishing centres of the British Isles. The blending of Scotch whisky must not be forgotten for it is responsible for the inflow to this country of millions of foreign currency. Numerous smaller firms in countless ancillary industries help to make up the industrial life of Edinburgh.

Port of Leith

The Port of Leith still retains its own name although part of the City of Edinburgh. The name comes from the stream, the Leith Water, which enters the sea through the docks. In the year 1389 King Robert the Bruce granted Edinburgh a charter conveying to that City the Harbour and Mills of Leith. For the next 500 years this charter continued in force, although Leith, as a Burgh, was a separate entity; then in 1838 the docks were transferred to the Commissioners for the Harbour and Docks of Leith. In 1920 the Burgh of Leith was absorbed by the City of Edinburgh while the Harbour and Docks remained with the Commissioners; in 1967 this arrangement ended and the Burgh of Leith became wholly a part of Edinburgh but keeps its own name.

Queensferry

Eight miles west of Edinburgh centre is the old port of Queensferry, now known chiefly for the two magnificent bridges, the Forth railway bridge, completed in 1890 and starting from Dalmeny, and the new road bridge, opened in 1964, which takes off from Queensferry itself rather like an aerial trapeze and in complete contrast to the Forth bridge, which must be counted among the wonders of engineering. From many points in the Pentland Hills and from any high spot in the nearby countryside or from Edinburgh itself, the Forth Bridges can be seen, the older one a magnificent monument of the early days. The coastline of Edinburgh City, which covers nine miles of the Firth of Forth, is, as one would expect, built up and partly industrialised. From west to east it includes Cramond, with the remains of the Roman Fort at the mouth of the Almond River, Granton and Granton Harbour, Newhaven with its harbour and, of course, Leith, the Port of Edinburgh. Then comes the very old town of Portobello and a few one-time villages alongside the western bank of the River Esk. From Leith to the Esk there are some good sandy beaches, and Portobello is considered a seaside resort. Fisherrow, nearest to the mouth of the Esk, is an old village with a tiny harbour that for centuries was entirely self-contained and cherished its own traditions and ways of life; as long ago as the eighteenth century only half a dozen boats fished from Fisherrow, but this tiny port was the landing-place for the fishing vessels from far afield to land their catches for the Edinburgh market. Newhaven, just west of Leith, was another harbour with similar traditions. However, both Granton and Newhaven were small ports handling cargo for Edinburgh in a small way, for Leith has always been the port for Edinburgh.

Open Hills

Immediately south of the City are the Pentland Hills. In fact, Edinburgh is partly built on the foothills of the Pentlands and so has, right at its doorstep, an area of open hills and lochs extending to many, many square miles and climbing to little less than 2,000 feet. Roads run closely around this wide open space and footpaths cross and re-cross these lovely hills.

Musselburgh

Population: 17,249.
Early Closing Day: Thursday.

Musselburgh gets its name from the mussel beds lying off the mouth of the River Esk, on both sides of which the town, or Burgh, straggles for close on two miles; the western side comprises the one-time village of Fisherrow. The local people will tell you that Musselburgh was a Royal Burgh before Edinburgh, and this might well be true, for it has been a Royal Burgh since the reign of King David I, and it is doubtful whether Edinburgh can claim a more ancient distinction than that; be that as it may, Musselburgians are proud of their town and their history. Probably the most distinguished and attractive building is the Tolbooth, which has quite clearly been inspired by the architecture of the Dutch, with whom this coast had close trading relations for several centuries.

Market Gardens

A fishing-net factory, started very early in the last century is now one of the biggest in the United Kingdom. Another industry which has helped to bring prosperity to Musselburgh is wire rope making. Inland from Musselburgh, and in East Lothian generally, the land is rich and has been famous for its market gardens since the Monks of Newbattle Abbey first instructed the people in the art of vegetable growing; today a large proportion of Edinburgh's vegetables are grown in East Lothian.

Salt Pans

This is a low and sandy shore and fortunately the A1 with its noisy traffic by-passes all the little coastal towns and villages until Musselburgh is reached. So that Prestonpans, though today only a relic of its prosperous past, can be explored in peace and comfort. In the twelfth century the Monks of Newbattle worked the salt pans here, hence the suffix pans. The industry was refounded in the seventeenth century and prospered until the repeal of the salt duty in 1825. Excellent clay for pottery-making was another discovery of the busy Monks and this led, by the eighteenth century, to the establishment of another prosperous industry. Coal-mining was another ancient industry now replaced by the huge generating station.

Nearby is the site of the Battle of Prestonpans, fought on 21 September 1745, a victory for Bonnie Prince Charlie.

First Railway

Around the next blunt headland are the two one-time fishing ports of Cockenzie and Port Seton. Their comparative prosperity continued until after the Second World War although Cockenzie still has a boat-building yard and some thirty boats. The first railway in Scotland was built in 1772, with wooden rails, to carry coals from Tranent to Cockenzie. A right of way follows this line to Tranent Church. Today the two villages form one burgh and a popular holiday resport, with Seton sands sheltered by obtrusions of rock and a footpath to the remains of Seton Castle and Elphinstone Tower, which is an Ancient Monument.

Longniddry

Here there is a rocky ledge which is excellent for diving. The beach here is not too crowded and can be reached by a very pleasant walk from the village. For most of the short journey from Longniddry to Aberlady the road is close to the sea coast, with some fine views along the Firth of Forth to Edinburgh, Prestonpans and across to Fife. This

is a first-class place to picnic alongside the car. A footpath follows
the coast around the golf-course to the Nature Reserve and Aberlady
Bay.

Aberlady

Aberlady lies at the head of an extensive bay which is a Nature
Reserve and the home of myriads of sea birds. Westwards are
Craigielaw Point, Gosford Sands in Gosford Bay and Seton Sands;
so that this coast can offer a good deal more than most people would
suppose. Aberlady was once the port for Haddington, some five or six
miles to the south, and is, today, a very attractive village with some
splendid views along the southern shore of the Firth of Forth to the
Castle and spires of Edinburgh which, with the sun setting behind this
silhouette of the Capital City, is an unforgettable picture. It should be
noted that Aberlady Bay is not suitable for children or for swimming.
The best entrance to the Bay is by the footbridge at the east end of the
village or from Gala Law Quarry, where the main road crosses the
Gullane Links. The nearby Luffness Tower House of the sixteenth
century should be seen.

Golf Courses

Gullane, Goolan, or, as in days gone by, Golyn was early in the
seventeenth century merged with the Parish of Dirleton, thus leaving
the Parish Church of Gullane, which is largely twelfth century, with
a Norman chancel arch, to disintegrate; this is now the nicest part of
what is largely a new village. Although Gullane is a mile from the sea
it is a popular resort especially with golfers, for there are five courses.
The magnificent stretch of sand along the gentle curve of Gullane Bay
makes this the finest beach in East Lothian.

Castle of Dirleton

Two and a half miles east of Gullane, and hidden from the sea by a
belt of woodland, are the village and Castle of Dirleton. This is a gem
of a village centred around the village green with some fine gardens
and a screen of great trees. Close by are the Castle gates, leading to
the gardens, the ancient yew trees and the seventeenth-century
bowling green. The Castle of Dirleton was the stronghold of the de
Vaux family and retains a group of thirteenth-century towers believed
to be one of the earliest examples of a clustered donjon; other remains
are from the fourteenth, fifteenth, and sixteenth centuries. A footpath
runs down to the sea at Yellowcraig from where Fidra Island and
lighthouse can be seen. The visitor can walk along the Broad Sands to
North Berwick or westwards along the rockier beach to Gullane.

NORTH BERWICK

Population: 4,450.
Early Closing Day: Thursday.

THE TWO MOST NOTABLE FEATURES of North Berwick are the Bass Rock and the conical Law behind the town which rises to about 640 feet and is topped with a whalebone arch, a relic of the Dunbar whaling fleet of bygone days. The greatest attraction of this whinstone plug is the wonderful view from its summit. The Bass Rock lies three miles from North Berwick and about one and a half miles from the coast at its nearest point. As might be expected this is the home of countless thousands of sea birds, particularly the Gannets or Solan Geese, also Razorbills, Puffins, Eider Duck and many other species. Bass Rock is a Nature Reserve.

Bass Rock

The rock itself rises about 350 feet with almost sheer sides, is about a mile in circumference and, from east to west, has a natural tunnel which is only accessible at low tide. Half-way up the Rock are the ruins of a pre-Reformation chapel that was dedicated to St. Baldred and consecrated in 1542. Weather permitting, launches will take visitors to the Bass Rock daily but permits must be obtained in order to land on the Rock. In 1902 a lighthouse was built and a fog-horn was installed high up on the northern side.

Tantallon Castle

White Lady of Fidra

Fidra Island, the most westerly of the four islands off North Berwick, is a very short distance from the mainland. It again has a lighthouse and is shaped rather like a horseshoe ; under the northern arm of this horseshoe, and well above sea-level, is a tunnel or perforation which, when seen from a particular point, looks rather like a female figure in a veil. This has become known as the White Lady of Fidra. At the southern end, on a flat knoll, are some ruins of the Castle of Tarbert. In Gaelic Tairbeart means a peninsula. The above particulars about Fidra originated in a guide to North Berwick dated 1911.

Priory

The Royal Burgh of North Berwick is now a popular and growing holiday resort, blending old with new and with a dry and temperate climate to recommend it. The harbour, with North Berwick Law is as pleasant and picturesque as most little harbours; the town is friendly and welcoming with a certain Victorian respectability, attracting many of the older generations. Near the Harbour, on the Auld Kirk Green, are the remains of the pre-Reformation Parish Church of North Berwick, dedicated to St. Andrew. The Abbey or, more correctly, the Priory in Old Abbey Road, is all that is left of the Cistercian Nuns Monastery or Priory, which was founded in the twelfth century. Several interesting fragments may be seen in the Burgh Museum.

Rocky inlets

Altogether North Berwick is one of those—now few and far between —peaceful, quiet and friendly places that bring the visitor back year after year.

At North Berwick we leave the Firth of Forth and face the North Sea: and from here southwards the coast scenery changes into a series of tiny rocky inlets, one or two larger ones and few stretches of golden sand. Inland, westwards the rich agricultural land stretches away to Edinburgh and the Pentland Hills, southwards to the rolling and lovely heather-covered Lammermuirs.

Tantallon Castle

Three miles south of North Berwick is one of the finest castles in Scotland, Tantallon. The best view of Tantallon is from the little horseshoe shaped cove south of the Castle ; turn left at Auldhame and follow the side road through a wooded dene to the sea, walk north along the coast to the northern point of the bay and then will be seen Tantallon high overhead like a fairy castle in a childhood story. This Castle, the home of the mighty Douglases, was in existence in 1374.

It was built in an almost impregnable situation with the sheer cliffs and the sea on three sides, across the fourth a vast curtain wall was built outside of which a deep trench was constructed with but one entrance, over a drawbridge. On the seaward side there was apparently a sea entrance, and some slight remains of what may have been a jetty are said to be visible at low tide. To savour the full flavour of Tantallon Scott's *Marmion* should be read. Tantallon Castle is in the care of the Dept. of Env. and is open to the public. The little half-moon shaped bay south of Tantallon, mentioned above, is a delightful spot for leisure and picnics; it is unlikely to be crowded.

Tithe Barn

At Whitekirk, three miles farther south, is the very beautiful red stone pre-Reformation Kirk of St. Mary's. This little church is authoritatively held to be the finest example of the early Gothic Parish Churches in Scotland. Behind it is one of the rare and very old tithe barns.

DUNBAR

Population: 4,600.
Early Closing Day: Wednesday.

A S WITH SO MANY PLACES in Southern Scotland, and particularly in the south-east, Dunbar's history and development has been largely bound up with her nearness to, and relations with, the Auld Enemy, at least until the complete amalgamation of the two countries in 1707. Undoubtedly Dunbar's history began a long time before England and Scotland were known by those names, but very little, if anything, is known of those early days. The most surprising thing one learns when delving into history is that Dunbar became a port only comparatively recently. Until 1655 there was a quay for small fishing vessels only. This was severely damaged in a gale and Cromwell's government was persuaded to spend three hundred pounds on the pier to the east, thus forming the Old Harbour. At that time all shipping, other than small fishing craft, used the harbour at Belhaven, a couple of miles to the west. The new Victoria Harbour was not constructed until 1842, for even with the help of the new pier the old harbour was dangerous, the rocks around the mouth making an entrance for larger ships very hazardous. Shortly after the Victoria Harbour was built the railway came, and within a few years Dunbar's great coastal trade lapsed and dwindled away, until today both harbours are used by a few fishing craft only. In the same way, Belhaven, for several hundred years the port of Dunbar, has died.

Castle Ruins

The ruins of the once great and powerful Castle on the headland, through which the seaway was cut to the Victoria Harbour, was first constructed sometime prior to 849, for in that year it was burned by the Macalpines; it is highly probable that at that time it was a wooden fort. In 1333 the Earl of Dunbar himself had the Castle destroyed so that the English could not take possession. However, Edward III, who had just won the Battle of Halidon Hill (1333), forced him to rebuild it at his own expense, thereafter garrisoning it with English troops. In 1435 the Castle became a Royal residence until its destruction in 1568. During the last four hundred and two years the sea and the weather between them have wrought havoc, but the ruins still fascinate if only by their sea girt and majestic position.

East Beach

The Royal Burgh of Dunbar is today a jolly and a friendly town with most of the adjuncts of the modern seaside holiday. East Beach, to the east of the town, is fine for children, while the two harbours, the promenades, the ruins of the Castle and westwards the sands of Belhaven will provide amusements for all. The countryside around, especially the Lammermuir Hills, will provoke the interest of those who prefer the peace and quietness of the lonelier places.

Dunbar House

The oldest building in Dunbar is the Town House, on the corner of Silver Street and High Street. Probably built around the early 1600's, it still serves the same purpose, the housing of the Council Chambers, the rooms that once served as a prison, and the public library. The tower, which is most attractive, houses a clock as well as a sundial, and the bell which still rings the ancient curfew at eight o'clock every evening. Dunbar House, known sometimes as Lauderdale House, which faces the Castle Park, is a striking remnant of the great days of Dunbar's sea-borne trade. It is worth noting that this very pleasant town has an exceptionally good record in the matter of health. During the Napoleonic Wars barracks were built here and troops have been stationed at Dunbar ever since. In a history of Dunbar, dated 1859, the excellent health of the troops is remarked upon.

Barns Ness Lighthouse

At the most southerly point of the town, and right on the coast, is a footpath along the coast to Barns Ness Lighthouse; a return can be made by Broxburn or by East Barns. There are many delightful walks within easy distance of Dunbar. The coast from Dunbar to Thorntonloch is one of the most interesting stretches from a geological viewpoint; a booklet is published entitled *Barns Ness*, which deals with this in a most interesting and detailed manner. Some very fine views are to be had from near Barns Ness Lighthouse.

Battlefields

Two battles have been fought at Dunbar. In the first, in 1296, Edward I of England overcame the Scots under John Baliol. This battle took place to the south of the town. The second, and better known conflict, took place to the east of the town on 3 September, 1650, when Oliver Cromwell's Roundheads defeated the Scots. There is a memorial on the main road near Oxwellmains and not far from the present-day cement works, which have been built on the eastern part of the battlefield.

Smugglers Cove

Southwards from Dunbar the coast gets a lot more rugged and picturesque, with cove after cove and headland after headland. The Great North Road keeps fairly close to the sea as it passes through, or close to, several not particularly interesting villages. The only village on this stretch of coast that nestles by the sea is Thorntonloch, a pleasant little place. The old Lothian–Berwick boundary is crossed and then comes Cockburnspath, which has a church with a most unusual round tower, and a very ancient market cross. Close to this village, with the look of the coaching days, is a cove and tiny harbour known locally as Smugglers Cove. This is a remarkable little spot, for the tiny harbour cannot be reached from land except by a cave in the high cliffs : another cave is said to lead to the hotel at Cockburnspath, a most fascinating and delightful spot that may well have been the haunt of smugglers. Just before entering Cockburnspath the A1 turns towards the west, while a side road continues southwards along the coast—this is by far the most interesting road and it rejoins the A107 about two and a half miles farther on. Although a number of tracks and footpaths lead down to the coast on a particularly rugged and interesting reach, the motorist must keep inland through Coldingham, where the ancient Priory should be visited. Turn left or north-east here for the little port and lifeboat station of St. Abbs.

Wolf's Crag

This is a really delightful and largely unspoiled village with the smell of the sea and the atmosphere as well. It occupies a tiny cove on a coastline of really rugged beauty. Probably the finest walk in the immediate area is to St. Abbs Head, over a stretch of lovely moorland with two little unnamed lochs and the sea never more than a quarter of a mile away. Visitors are welcomed at the lighthouse on the Head,

Edinburgh skyline, with Scott Monument

River Tweed. near Coldstream

Smugglers' Cove Harbour, Cockburnspath

but the most entrancing views and the myriads of sea birds combined with the wild remoteness of the situation is the finest reward. Three miles north of St. Abbs Head is Fast Castle, Wolf's Crag of Sir Walter Scott's *Bride of Lammermoor*. Very little of the Castle remains but the position is superb. On a rocky headland in an isolated and extremely rugged piece of coast this Castle can only be entered at one point by a narrow drawbridge, a fascinating and romantic situation for a castle. The finest way to approach Fast Castle is along the cliff-top from the north or south. A footpath follows the coast southwards to Eyemouth, a distance of three to four miles along an enchanting piece of rock-girt coastline.

Eyemouth

Population: 2,269.
Early Closing Day: Thursday.

The little coastal town of Eyemouth is delightfully situated at the head of Eyemouth Bay at the mouth of the River Eye. The harbour is a busy and most interesting spot. The town itself is a nice clean attractive place. Not a great deal remains of old Eyemouth, which was a port of more than ordinary complexity. Narrow wynds, the houses built in clusters, a marked division between the fishing and agricultural sections, many underground passages and a vast and prosperous smuggling trade made of Eyemouth, prior to the nineteenth century, a quite unusual and very original fishing village. Gunsgreen House was the centre and headquarters of this trade, which assumed massive proportions in the sixteenth and seventeenth centuries. As early as 1214 Eyemouth had a harbourmaster and the trade to warrant the appointment. To a greater or lesser extent this sea trade, largely coastal, continued until the coming of the railways. From the very earliest days fishing has been, perhaps, the major source of income for the people of Eyemouth, this culminating in the prosperous years of the nineteenth century, which were terminated suddenly and tragically in 1881, when a violent storm destroyed twenty-three fishing boats and took with them one hundred and twenty-three of the men of Eyemouth. Black Friday, or Disaster Day, was 14 October, 1881, and as might be expected it left an indelible mark on the town. In spite of years when the fishing industry suffered depression between the two world wars, Eyemouth is still a large fishing port looking forward to a very prosperous future. For well over a hundred years boat building, particularly fishing boats, has been carried on at Eyemouth, and today other light industries contribute to the industrial life of this energetic little town.

Hawk's Nest

Eyemouth had a fort but very little of this remains today. As with a number of castles and forts near the border with England, many of these were subject to demolishing and rebuilding, often more than once. Of greater interest to the visitor will be the attractions that Eyemouth offers. A beautiful coast, a lovely countryside, a week of festivities connected with the Crowning of the Herring Queen, a colourful and interesting harbour, and most of the amenities to be expected in a very small seaside town. The area abounds in glorious walks among which the cliff-top path southwards to Burnmouth, which passes over Hawk's Nest, the highest cliff on the mainland of Great Britain, is particularly to be recommended. Burnmouth is another delightful little village. In many places along this wonderful coast the beautiful red sandstone is much in evidence; the whole coastline to Dunbar is a wonderland of tiny bays and hidden coves, of fantastic rock formations, of magnificent scenery with only the noise of the sea and the wind, and the call of the sea birds; to lovers of nature this is one of the finest coast-lines to be found. Three miles more of this same fascinating coast and the English—Scottish border is reached between a tiny cove named Meg's Dub and Marshall Meadows Bay.

HADDINGTON

Population: 6,700.
Early Closing Day: Thursday. Last Thursday in each month is a holiday.
Market Days: Monday, Friday.

HADDINGTON IS NOT ONLY the main town of East Lothian but one of the most outstanding towns within easy reach of Edinburgh It has been called the Adam Town, for that great architect was responsible for many of the finest eighteenth-century houses of which Haddington has a number. It is fortunate that the authorities have seen fit to renovate and preserve many of these fine houses. Another piece of good fortune that befell Haddington was the fact that, in the railway boom of the early years of last century, Haddington was by-passed by the main line and missed the tremendous building programmes that spoiled so many railway towns. Haddington is an Adam Town of distinction and charm. The wide streets and sense of plenty of room adds to its general attractiveness, while the River Tyne (not to be confused with the better known Tyne over the border in Northumberland) which winds around two sides of the town, provides pleasant footpath walks and much lovely scenery.

Lamp of the Lothians

Haddington has been a Royal Burgh since the days of King David I and certainly since 1130. It has also been the home of kings. The oldest building and the most moving is the twelfth- or thirteenth-century Abbey Church of St. Mary, which is one of the finest and largest pre-Reformation churches in Scotland. Built largely of the typically Scottish dark red sandstone, it stands very close to the River Tyne in an open area that sets the seal of age and beauty on this south-east corner of the town. Although the choir and transepts are in ruins, the 90-foot tower is complete, and the nave and western part of the cruciform is still used as the Parish Church. For long the fine old Abbey has been known as Lucerna Londoniae, the Lamp of the Lothians. The best buildings in the town are Carlyle House, the home of the town council; the National Commercial Bank of Scotland, the Bank of Scotland House and Jane Welsh's House. Among the other features that should be seen are the quaint old shop-signs in High Street and the Mercat Cross. The Victoria and the Nungate bridges can be seen as part of a pleasant riverside walk that takes in the Abbey, the medieval Abbey Bridge and Lady Kitty's Garden, as well as the waterside buildings and old mills. Haddington House of 1680 is being renovated and preserved.

Agricultural Land

East Lothian being very largely an agricultural, and indeed a very rich agricultural, land, the industries of Haddington have always had a strong agricultural tie-up. The first Farmers Club was founded here in 1743. Potatoes were introduced to East Lothian in 1754 and have since become a famous crop, more especially the early variety. In 1787 Andrew Meikle, a mechanic's son, invented the threshing machine. Knitwear and hosiery are the two chief industrial occupations of Haddington, apart from the very important mills and maltings. Agricultural machinery and its servicing naturally takes a very important place in the town's activities.

The centre and eastern sections of East Lothian have been given over almost entirely to agriculture, barley, potatoes and market gardening.

Natural Boundary

The county of East Lothian is one of the smaller ones in Scotland, yet agriculturally it is one of the richest; it has also produced its share of history-makers, of people who are largely responsible for the

Scotland of today. It is bounded on the north by the sea, on the south by Berwickshire and on the west by Midlothian. Although Berwickshire forms the southern boundary, it is in fact the heights of the Lammermuirs that make the entirely natural boundary. Within this quite small section of country there is a wealth of glorious scenery, a host of interesting places and many old castles and churches.

Dunbar Common

Starting at the south-eastern corner, we have already followed the coast. Dunbar Common and the northernmost of the Lammermuirs cover a large area and are a delight for walkers, and even the motorist can view some of the beauties, many rarely seen, if he is prepared to explore the side roads and little tracks that enter these hills for at least a mile or two. A road from Dunbar through Spott and Thurston Mains, from Innerwick and Oldhamstocks, from Stenton and all the little villages along the northern foothills of the Lammermuirs will take the motorist well into these lovely hills with their scores of burns and rivers. From Garvald and from Gifford these hills may be crossed to their southern boundary, and what scenery these two roads offer! Right and left of the roads are for walkers only.

Priory of Nunraw

There are three villages in the foothills of the Lammermuirs that are worthy of a special visit. Gifford, about four miles south of Haddington, is of very special interest on account of Yester House and gardens; it is not open to the public but permission may be obtained to walk through the grounds to visit the Goblin Ha' and the ruined castle which features in Scott's *Marmion*, The village has a golf-course and, if not of special interest, is pleasant enough. It is a planned village with some interest for architects. Gervald is on the main road from Dunbar to Gifford and about seven or eight miles from Dunbar. Built of old red sandstone it is a delightful and picturesque village. High above the village is the Cistercian Priory of Nunraw, where a new Abbey is being built by the monks themselves. Visitors are always welcome and no enquiries appear to be made as to their religion. Stenton, some six miles from Dunbar, is a delightful straggling little village that takes one's mind back into the days of horses; it sits in a delightful situation among the woods and burns where spring and early summer are the best seasons. East Linton is, perhaps, the most impressive of the villages of East Lothian, impressive because of its watermill at next door Preston. This is the property of the Scottish National Trust, and is a most interesting example of how man, not so long ago, carried out his milling operations. It is still operated for visitors, and is also a really delightful spot from the artistic viewpoint. East Linton is a Burgh and it takes its name from the rocky linn in the River Tyne which is spanned by an ancient and picturesque bridge.

Traprain Law

Two miles south-west of East Linton is the remarkable hill of Traprain Law, from where some first-class views can be had. Of no great height Traprain yet stands prominently on a flattish landscape and is the more outstanding for that reason. In pre-Roman days Traprain must have supported a camp of some importance, for from this hill has come some of the richest hauls of bronze, silver and pottery unequalled. Most of these treasures are in the National Museum of Antiquities.

Hailes Castle

From East Linton a riverside footpath leads to Hailes Castle, which can be reached by road. As with Yester and Dirleton Castles there is a great deal of thirteenth-century work to be seen at Hailes, much of it in fine order. Hailes occupies a glorious position on the River Tyne and, apart from its historical interest, is well worth a visit. Another magnificent house and grounds that must be mentioned is Lennoxlove, the home of the Duke of Hamilton; this can be visited by arrangement only.

Humble

South-west from Haddington runs the A6093, giving a continuous view of the Lammermuirs while on the east side of the Tyne the A6137 passes the village of Bolton, where the mother of Robert Burns is buried and continues to the most attractive village of Humble at the very foothills of some of the steepest of the Lammermuirs and only a short distance from Soutra Summit. At Humble is a children's village consisting of separate houses donated by separate benefactors.

Fenton Tower

North of Haddington are the small but pleasant Garleton Hills, north-east of which is Athelstaneford. From the summit of the Garletons some fine views can be had in all directions. Athelstaneford is a planned village built on a rocky outcrop with pantiled cottages on both sides of a street distinguished by its grass verges. About three to four miles north of Athelstaneford is the hamlet of Kingston, on another outcrop, and with a ruined sixteenth-century tower house, Fenton Tower.

A little to the west lies Drem, distinguished as the railway junction for North Berwick.

Duns

Population: 2,000.
Early Closing Day: Wednesday.
Tourist Information Office: Burgh Chambers.

Duns once the county town of Berwickshire, is a pleasant little place dating from 1558 when the old town on the south-western slope of Duns Law was destroyed by English forces. The present town is situated at the foot of the southern slope of Duns Law. The name is said to mean hill or fort, from the Celtic. As with all Border towns, Duns suffered from the continuous raid and counter-raid during the centuries of intermittent warfare. Old Duns was almost surrounded by impenetrable marshland with but one road through, and this road was guarded by a fort or Barmykin; the present Barmykin Hotel stands where, it is believed, this fort was sited. In 1489 Duns was granted a charter by James IV, and assumed the status of a Burgh of Barony. Probably the most impressive single feature of the town is the public park with the ancient Mercat Cross. This is an unusually fine and well-kept park for a town the size of Duns.

Summer Festival

The most important event in the town's calendar is the Summer Festival held in the first full week in July. The chief figures are the Reiver and the Reiver's Lass. The Reiver of days gone by was a figure sometimes of romance, sometimes of fame and renown but more often of fear, certainly on the other side of the Border, for there were both English and Scottish Reivers. The week's festivities include church services and every kind of jollity, as well as visits to the Laird of Duns Castle and other mansions. Children take a big part in much of the week's fun. Duns Castle is just outside the Burgh and is a handsome, almost magnificent, building, incorporating many periods but retaining one part of the original, the fourteenth-century eastern tower. Close to the Castle is a lake, known locally as the Hen Poo'. This is a sanctuary for wild fowl and many types of birds. West of the Castle are the ruins of Borthwick Castle, not to be confused with the much larger and more ornate Borthwick Castle in Midlothian. This one was in all probability a tower or gate-house to Duns Castle. Permits can be obtained from the Estate Office in Market Square to walk through the Castle grounds and around the lake.

Trout Rivers

The County of Berwick, in which Duns occupies a nearly central position, is bounded by the Lammermuirs to the north, the sea to the

east, the Vale of Merse, or the Tweed Valley, to the south and the
beautiful Lauderdale to the west. From the Tweed to the Lammermuirs
is rich agricultural land, chiefly so in the Tweed Valley. The coast
we have seen and the Dale of Lauder in its rich hill-guarded
loveliness we shall shortly visit. One of the finest runs in Berwickshire
is along the famous Tweed Valley, from Kelso to Berwick on Tweed
through the interesting town of Coldstream. Another is from Kelso
through Duns to cross the Lammermuirs into East Lothian and
Haddington, or alternatively to follow Lauderdale across the western
approaches to the Lammermuirs and so to Edinburgh. One other point
should be noted about Berwickshire—it is possibly the finest area for
fishing in Southern Scotland. Duns lies midway, two to three miles
from each, between the Blackadder and the Whitadder, and both are
famous trout rivers. In addition there is the Tweed, world famous, the
tributaries of all three Rivers and the Eye. Then there is the Watch
Water Reservoir some eight miles west of Duns. Permits can be
obtained from the Rathburne Hotel, Longformacus, for boat fishing
only, and excellent trout have been taken here.

From Kelso, which will be dealt with in the section on the Borders,
follow the River Tweed north-eastwards through some of the most
beautiful scenery. The road follows the river closely to Coldstream.

Coldstream

Population: 1,500.
Early Closing Day: Thursday.
Tourist Information Office: High Street.

This very clean open little town sits right on the banks of the Tweed
and opposite Cornhill-on-Tweed. The Burgh of Coldstream gave its
name to the Coldstream Guards when, in 1659, General Monk used
Coldstream as his winter headquarters. There was a Cistercian Priory
here, founded in the twelfth century, and after many vicissitudes it was
finally dissolved in 1621. The Majoribanks Monument in the town
commemorates the first Member of Parliament for Berwickshire after
the passing of the Reform Act in 1832. At nearby Lennel are the ruins
of a church believed to have been founded by the nuns of Coldstream
Priory; it was the Parish Church until 1718. It is described by Sir Walter
Scott in *Marmion*. Between three and four miles north of Coldstream
on the road to Swinton is the very tiny place named Simprint; here
there is another ruined church and graveyard. At Ladykirk is one of the
oldest churches in this region. It was built by James IV early in the
sixteenth century, but there must have been an earlier church for the
first preacher is given as of 1159. This church is unusual in that it

has a stone slab roof. It stands right opposite Norham Castle in Northumberland.

Dundock Wood

Some two miles west of Coldstream are Dundock Wood and Hirsel Lake. These grounds are freely open to the public but no picnicking is allowed; the woods and lake are preserved as a bird sanctuary. This is a very beautiful estate with some fine timber and much wild-life; care should be taken to observe strictly the *Country Code*. A few miles farther on, at a point some three miles before entering Berwick-on-Tweed, which is, of course, in England, the border turns north and within five or six miles reaches the sea.

Home Castle

West of Duns, along the foothills of the beautiful Lammermuirs and southwards to the border with Roxburghshire, are several lovely little places and much delightful country. About four miles south-west of Duns on the Greenlaw road is the very tiny village of Polwarth, with a church going back to A.D. 900. In 1242 a new chruch was dedicated to St. Mungo. This was rebuilt in 1378 and again in 1703, with the addition of the tower. The key to the church can be obtained from the inn or from the manse. This is quite an outstanding old church and very well worth a visit. Next comes Greenlaw, of no particular interest, but a great angling centre on the Blackadder, with Home Castle a dominating feature on a crag three miles away. Then comes Gordon, which in many ways is an outstanding village. The first noticeable thing will be the Free Church, with an unusual round tower dated 1893, and the Church, 1843. A mile or so west of the town is the fine old Border tower of Greenknowe, and opposite is Gordon Moss a Scottish Wildlife Trust Nature Reserve. Southwards from Gordon leads the visitor into Roxburghshire in a very few miles. South-west, about eight miles from Gordon, is Earlston, the site of Rhymer's Tower, which is in the charge of the Edinburgh Border Castles Association.

Thomas the Rhymer

This was the home of the famous Thomas the Rhymer. Earlston is on the Leader Water and the famous and exceptionally beautiful Lauderdale; not far north are the Lammermuir Hills, and but three miles to the south, the Tweed, with all the natural beauties that name conjures up. So let us journey up Lauderdale with the gentle hills on either hand and the high Lammermuirs growing more distinct to the north-east. We could have taken a road direct from Duns to Lauder, skirting closely the feet of the Lammermuirs, and for lovers of hills this is to be recommended.

Lauder

Population: 700.
Early Closing Day: Thursday.

Although Lauder is a very tiny place with a population of only 623, it deserves rather more notice than most villages of that size. It is a Royal Burgh and the only one in Berwickshire. The Charter was granted in the reign of William the Lion, 1165–1214. The town, for such must be called a Royal Burgh, has a deal of history behind it and many Royal visits. The hero of one historical story has been immortalised in Scott's *Marmion*. The Church and the Tolbooth, or Town Hall, are close together and form a very Scottish picture indeed. In front of the Tolbooth is the Mercat Cross, which bears the date 12-- ; the last two figures are unreadable. The Parish Church was removed from the Castle in 1673 by Act of Parliament and is built in the form of a Greek cross. Thirlstane Castle is the most imposing building for many miles around and was once the home of the Earl of Lauderdale. The age of the present building is difficult to determine but no doubt covers many periods. The old dungeons are still preserved with some instruments of torture. Until the sixteenth century it was known as Lauder Fort. Although the Castle is not open to the public, organised parties are shown over by arrangement with the Estates Office, Lauder. This is one of the most magnificent buildings. There was an older Thirlstane Castle and the ruins can be seen in a field on Eastmains Farm, close to the Boon Water, some three miles east of Lauder.

Good Fishing

North-east, north-west and due north of Lauder are the Lammermuir Hills, the haven of hill walkers and those who prefer the peace and quiet of nature. The foothills and the many streams provide much good fishing for which Duns, Greenlaw and Lauder are good centres.

Mecca for Artists

The journey up the Lauderdale should be taken quietly for there is much of real beauty as the road climbs the westward hills of the Lammermuirs, finally topping Soutra Summit at 1,208 feet close to the junction of Berwickshire, Midlothian and East Lothian. (The actual highest summit of the range is Meikle Says Law (1,750 feet), 12 miles to the E.N.E. of Soutra on the East Lothian border.) There is a secondary road from Duns that travels right across the centre of the Lammermuirs through the truly delightful village of Longformacus, a mecca for artists and painters. There is a church here that was founded

in 1243 and the situation of the village in a tiny wooded valley in
the hills would be very difficult to duplicate. This road continues over
the county boundary to Garvald or Gifford. At the southern tip of
Lauderdale, facing across the Tweed and the county boundary with
that small piece of Roxburghshire that separates Berwickshire from
Selkirkshire, is one of the best-known Border Abbeys, Dryburgh;
however, this is so close to the large places of Melrose and St.
Boswells in Roxburghshire that it will be more convenient to visit
Dryburgh from those places.

Soutra Summit

   The Lammermuirs, those glorious heather-covered hills, deserve a
word to themselves. Many years before the Great North Road became
the main highway into Scotland the Roman Dere Street crossed the
Border hills and continued north to Soutra Aisle and Soutra Summit,
and eventually to the Firth of Forth. Soutra is a place that probably
few people will have visited. However, every visitor to Southern
Scotland should stop where the A68 meets the B6368 and climb the
200 feet to the summit, from where a magnificent view of the whole
of the Firth of Forth and much of Edinburgh can be seen. When the
first Romans, who came this way, stood here and viewed the rich
lands of the Lothians, the mighty inlet of the Firth of Forth with its
good harbours and anchorages, they must indeed have seen this as a
very good northern boundary to their mighty Empire. One mile
southwards down the B6368 is Soutra Aisle, a tiny and very ancient
chapel close to where once stood an inn for the rest and refreshment
of travellers on this very heavy pull up, heavy whichever way the
traveller goes. Both Soutra Summit and Soutra Aisle are just within
Midlothian and can equally easily be visited from Edinburgh.

Viewpoints

   Roughly the Lammermuirs are bounded on the north by Dunbar and
Haddington, on the west by the A7 Edinburgh to Selkirk road, and on
the south by a line drawn from Lauder to Eyemouth. Within this area
there are virtually no towns, a few lovely little villages and miles and
miles of glorious hills crossed by a few roads and many old tracks,
green tracks that were busy roads in days gone by; one of these, the
Herring Road, runs from Dunbar to the Kelso and Melrose area and
along which the fisherwomen of Dunbar carried their creels of herring
for sale. Parts of this road can still be followed, parts are overgrown,
but an exploration of the whole of this track would make a worthwhile
walk. The Lammermuirs are among the safest of hills for amateur
walkers but it is well to be able to use a map and compass efficiently
before venturing forth. Use a detailed Ordnance Survey map. There are

many good high spots but Lammer Law (1,730 feet) and Meikle Says Law (1,750 feet) are two of the highest and are on the northern edge of the Lammermuirs. Both have trigonometrical points.

DALKEITH

Population: 9,150.
Early Closing Day: Tuesday. Some shops close all day on second Tuesday of each month.

SEVEN MILES SOUTH-EAST of Edinburgh, and only five miles from the sea at Musselburgh, is the fine and handsome town of Dalkeith As a dormitory to Edinburgh, as a centre of industrial activity, as a centre for the large surrounding district, Dalkeith performs a first-class service. Although there is much to be seen, much of interest and beauty, Dalkeith would not claim to be a holiday centre.

It is, as a matter of fact, situated in a particularly beautiful position on the junction of the North and South Esk Rivers in a land of winding streams and woodlands of great beauty. The outer environs of Edinburgh reach out to just about the latitude of Dalkeith, which has the effect of leaving Dalkeith as a beauty spot in, or close to, a land of housing estates and huge industrial areas. This is largely a Burgh, a Burgh of Barony, of new buildings, of modern services and open spaces, a place where business can be conducted in the freshness and pleasant atmosphere that we have come to expect. One or two old and very beautiful spots should not be forgotten.

Dalkeith Palace

At the northern end of High Street, are the gates to Dalkeith Palace. The original castle was rebuilt in the sixteenth century and in earlier days was a hunting seat for kings. Again it was rebuilt in the eighteenth century but the dining-room and one bedroom of the sixteenth-century palace remain, as well as many parts of the walls from 700 years ago. The eighteenth-century designs are attributed to Vanbrugh. The beautifully wooded grounds are laid out with a magnificent avenue of limes. Dalkeith Palace can be visited by arrangement. The North and South Esk meet very near the Palace with a fine view from the humpback bridge. Dalkeith is rich in parks and open spaces. Westgate Park is on the west side of the North Esk with its St. Mary's Chapel close to High Street. This Chapel is not of any great architectural note but adds to the charm of the immediate surroundings. Westgate Park, the property of the Duke of Buccleugh, contains many very old oak trees, the last vestiges of the Caledonian Forest. It is the scene of the Annual Show.

Woodland Walks

Other parks and open spaces give Dalkeith a very good share of the fresh air one would not expect so close to an industrial area. Footpaths, riverside and woodland walks enable the visitor thoroughly to enjoy the delights of the unusually beautiful countryside.

Newbattle Abbey

About a mile south of Dalkeith and close to the River South Esk in an outstandingly beautiful and well-wooded landscape is Newbattle Abbey. The original Cistercian foundation took place in 1140; of this only the crypt remains beneath one room of the very fine sixteenth-century house which was for a long time the seat of the Marquis of Lothian. Today this great house is the only adult residential college in Scotland. Melville Castle, to the south-west of Dalkeith, is in fact an eighteenth-century house now used as an hotel; it is a romantic looking place and stands in some lovely grounds.

Ford House

About five miles south-east of Dalkeith on the A68 is Ford House Pathhead; this is an exceptionally fine example of Scottish seventeenth-century architecture—the date 1680 is inscribed over the doorway. At the village of Carrington, five miles south of Dalkeith and two miles west of the A7, is the Parish Church of 1711, which replaced an earlier fifteenth-century church which had itself replaced a much earlier structure which had belonged to the Abbey of Scone in the twelfth century.

Blackhope Scar

The South Esk leads through many delightful villages, Carrington, Cockpen, Temple and on to the Roseberry and Gladhouse Reservoirs right at the feet of the Moorfoot Hills where Blackhope Scar (2,137 feet), is the source of the South Esk River on the boundary with Peeblesshire. Right in the south-east corner of the county, close to the B6458 and on a tiny side road, is Cakemuir Castle in the Lammermuir Hills; it is of fourteenth- or fifteenth-century origin and is said to have got its name from the hospitality offered to travellers on the road to Melrose.

Gore Water

Some five or six miles south of Dalkeith and a little east of the town of Gorebridge are two fine castles, Borthwick and Crichton. Borthwick consists almost entirely of two towers and is the largest pele tower in Scotland. It stands near the head waters of the Gore Water, a tributary of the South Esk, and is in fine condition, having suffered

little during its five hundred or so years of life. Crichton Castle sits
close to the headwaters of the Tyne and makes a very fine picture of
which Scott wrote

> That Castle rises on the steep
> Of the green vale of Tyne;
> And far beneath, where slow they creep
> From pool to eddy, dark and deep.
> Where alders moist, and willows weep.
> You hear her stream depine.

The first primitive tower was probably built in the thirteenth or
fourteenth century and additions made during the fifteenth. This is one
of the finest ruins in this part of Scotland and is in the care of the
Dept. of Environment, as is the equally glorious Borthwick. Crichton
Church is a pre-Reformation building (1448), which was never
completed, and this fact is easily seen. It was renovated at the end of
the nineteenth century.

Attractive Valleys

As one journeys through Midlothian one sees that only the Pentland
Hills, which reach right to the door of Edinburgh and give that great
City a playground such as few other cities can boast, relieve the
persistent overall industrial atmosphere. The Pentland Hills cut
Midlothian in half with the more rural areas to the east and the most
industrial to the west. The valleys of the North and South Esk, the
Water of Leith and the Pentland Hills are, however, very beautiful, and
give to Midlothian a holiday attraction she would not otherwise have.

Roslin Castle

The North Esk, which rises in Peeblesshire in the foothills of the
Pentlands, flows through some glorious wooded valleys with several
castle ruins and much very beautiful scenery. The A701 and the A702,
with the adjoining lanes, are the two roads which will enable the
visitor, coupled with a little map-reading, to explore this very lovely
valley and almost a part of the greater Edinburgh conurbation. Some
seven miles south of Edinburgh, very close to Roslin and right on the
banks of the North Esk, is the Castle of Hawthornden, which was
built in the fifteenth century, although it is said to be on the site of an
earlier castle that utilised the rocky bluff behind the present castle. It
is well worth a visit. A little south of Roslin in a most picturesque
setting alongside the river and above the glorious Roslin Glen is
Roslin Castle. Dating back to the fourteenth century, it is largely in
ruins, but its position is exceptional and must be seen to be
appreciated. Rosslyn Chapel, near Roslin Castle, is another of the
architectural glories of this part of South Scotland. It is of fifteenth-

century origin and is regarded as unique for the variety and beauty of its decorative carvings.

Show Pieces

Not far from the North Esk and about six or seven miles south of Edinburgh are two collieries, both regarded as the show pieces of Scotland in the coal-mining world. Ultra-modern and with a tremendous productive capacity, they should be well worth a visit.

Calder House

The Water of Leith, once famous for its water-mills, rises on the west side of the Pentland Hills and very soon enters the industrial areas. Between this stream and the old county boundary with West Lothian there are one or two places that are not far from the western slopes of the Pentland Hills and are still largely rural. Midcalder Parish Church is a sixteenth-century church on the site of an eleventh- or twelfth-century predecessor. Calder House, near Midcalder, is considered older than the village or the parish. The walls are in places, eight feet thick, and much of this fine old house will be thirteenth century or earlier. West of Edinburgh, between the A8 and the A71, is the village of Ratho, with a parish church which dates from the twelfth century; alterations have of course taken place since, but much of the original remains.

Moorfoot Hills

There are many places not mentioned in Midlothian, and most, if not all, are industrial in character; some have their beautiful and interesting features, but space does not permit of a complete and detailed examination. From Midlothian let us travel southwards into that wonderful land of Peeblesshire, a land of space a'plenty, of hills and fresh open country. Before we leave Midlothian let us not forget the great beauties, the magnificent views and many fine motor runs around the Pentland Hills and, most of all, the wonderful walks the fine hills afford for those who like to see the country on foot. Neither should we forget the Moorfoot Hills, which extend southwards into Peeblesshire.

Bow Castle

From the Gladhouse Reservoir on the South Esk River there is a rough track leading to Hirendean Castle, in ruins, in a wonderful open sweep of country at the foot of Blackhope Scar (2,137 feet) and just north of the Peeblesshire boundary. In this partly industrial county of Midlothian there is one other section of outstandingly lovely country which the A7 follows from Gorebridge shortly joining the Gala Water and following that lovely stream to Stow and other little villages, finally taking the motorist to Galashiels or east into Berwickshire. Three miles south of Stow is the tiny hamlet of Bow, with an outstanding hill to the east on the top of which are the remains of Bow Castle, making a most unusual and very outstanding picture with exceptional views. Two miles north of the village of Fountainhall on the A7 a road takes off north-eastwards; this is a quiet and very beautiful route to Soutra Summit and Soutra Aisle.

PEEBLES

Population: 6,000.
Early Closing Day: Wednesday.
Market Day: Friday.
Tourist Information Office: High Street.

QUITE APART FROM ITS SITUATION on the River Tweed (two-thirds of this beautiful river is in Peeblesshire). Peebles, a Royal and Ancient Burgh, is a place of many delights set in a countryside that would be difficult to improve upon. The town is a most pleasant and friendly place, a good shopping centre with one or two features of interest and beauty. Peebles' chief delight is the country around, for which this growing town is a fine centre.

Hay Lodge Park

The most outstanding feature of the town itself is Hay Lodge Park, alongside the River Tweed on the west side of the Auld Toon; this is a quite remarkably beautiful park that should not be missed. On the opposite side of the road at the main gates to Hay Lodge Park is St. Andrew's Tower, which marks the remains of St. Andrew's Church, the oldest architectural remains in Peebles and quite possibly in the county. It was founded in 1195, the tower being restored in 1882. The most moving architectural ruins in Pebbles is the Cross Kirk in St. Andrew's Road. This venerable place is believed to have been in existence as the burial place of St. Nicholas the Bishop, with a cross, in A.D. 296. None of this remains today but part of a church built upon the site and at various times known as Cross Kirk, Church of the Holy Cross, Church of St. Nicholas, the Church of the Redemptorists, and, lastly, the Abbey of the Trinity, "Callit the Croce Kirk". In medieval days there was a priory of Red Friars and it was the glory of medieval Peebles. Many of the relics of those ancient days are enshrined within the present Cross Kirk. When the Cross Kirk was finally abandoned as a church the Parish Church of St. Nicholas was built at the west end of High Street then known as Castle Hill; this was replaced in 1887.

Chambers Institution

In the High Street, is the Chambers Institution. Imposing in appearance, it is a great deal more ancient than it at first appears. It was in existence before 1624, when it belonged to the Cross Kirk, and was renovated and partly converted in 1859 into a Hall, Reading Room, Library and Museum. There is much of real interest inside. The Mercat Cross, where Eastgate and Northgate cross, is a very ancient piece of stone which has served Peebles, the Auld Toon, for hundreds of years.

Old Bridge

The Tweed bridge, which has been twice widened, is fifteenth century, and can be seen clearly from the west side.

Tweed

The chief industry of Peebles is the weaving of Tweed, an ancient trade that at one time derived its power from the waters of the river from which the material is said to get its name. The best way, and the only satisfactory way, to explore Peebles is to read the guide and then spend a day walking quietly with eyes open, for there is much that lack of space forbids the mention of.

Glentrees Forest

North-east of Peebles lies Glentrees Forest, an area of over 2,000 acres covering the foothills of the southern Moorfoot Hills that is largely open to the public. From the main Forest Office there are some miles of footpaths and grassy glades that are signposted so that the nature-lover can stroll without fear of getting lost. North and east of Peebles, between the A7 and the B709, are miles and miles of open hill country uncrossed by roads but a delight to the keen and experienced hill-walker. Here and there rough tracks run into these hills, enabling the adventurous motorist to try some unusual motoring and to see a countryside he would otherwise never see. A large number of these hills rise to close on 2,000 feet and make for fine exhilarating walking.

Eddleston Water

The A703 northwards from Peebles alongside the Eddleston Water is a picturesque road of many delights, but better still is the side road that heads for Eddleston from a point some three or four miles west of Peebles. On this road there are many fine places for picnicking. Both roads join at Eddleston, where the Horse Shoe Inn is worth a call. From here northwards the A703 continues its picturesque journey up the Eddleston Water to join the A701 and cross the county boundary into Midlothian at Leadburn.

Evening scene: Firth of Clyde

Traquair House: great and historic Scottish residence

Burns' Cottage, Alloway

Burns' characters; Souter Johnnie's Cottage, Kirkoswald

Innerleithen

Population: 2,286.
Early Closing Day: Tuesday.

Some six miles south east of Peebles, and still on the River Tweed, is Innerleithen, a small town of old grey stone and mills. There are two roads from Peebles, one north and one south of the river. Both are delightful, with high hills on either side, while the road, follows closely the ever-beautiful Tweed. Note the ruins of Horsbrugh Castle high up on the northern bank of the Tweed and a long way above the road. Innerleithen attained some sort of fame when it was discovered that the St. Ronan's Well had some health-giving properties, but it was Scott's novel, *St. Ronan's Well*, published in 1824, that really brought Innerleithen to life. Probably Innerleithen's greatest attraction is the countryside, the Tweed and the provision made by the authorities for short and most pleasant walks in and around the town. In addition, of course, the countryside is wide open for walkers and it should be noted that the country people of Scotland do welcome genuine and well-behaved walkers who obey the *Country Code*.

Leithen Water
   Innerleithen gives one the impression of having a hill at every street end, and in that respect is most unusual. The B709 northwards from Innerleithen which follows the Leithen Water over some of the wildest of the Moorfoot Hills crosses into Midlothian midway between the steepest of the hills at over 1,500 feet. This is a road for campers and caravanners, for there is plenty of room for both and scenery of the wildest and widest kind.

Stantling Reservoir
   On the north bank of the Tweed and a couple of miles east of Innerleithen is the little mill town of Walkerburn, in very beautiful Tweedside scenery; a little east of the town and south of the river are the very picturesque ruins of a castle or pele high on the hill-side. Some three miles east of Walkerburn is the tiny Tweedside village of Thornylea, from where a road, narrow but wholly peaceful, leads through good farming country, past the picturesque ruins of another pele on the far side of Stantling Reservoir, and after much lovely country, green and pleasant, reaches Stow on the Gala Water.

Traquair House
   South of the Tweed and close to both Peebles and Innerleithen are three forests, Cardrona, Elibank and Traquair. These forests add

immensely to the already great beauty of the Upper Tweed Valley.
About a mile south of Innerleithen is Traquair House, reputed to be the
most ancient house in Scotland that is still lived in. The beginnings
of Traquair House are not known with certainty. It is believed that
there was a house of wood here in A.D.950, when this area was deep
inside the Ettrick Forest. By 1107 there was a fairly substantial building
on this site and it certainly included the tower of the twentieth-century
Traquair. The name is said to originate with the British *tra*, a dwelling,
and *quair*, a stream. For many years during the medieval period
Traquair was at times a royal residence and during its long history has
changed hands many times. During the late seventeenth century it
became one of the great Catholic houses in a largely Protestant land.

Bear Gates

The family of Stuarts of Traquair have apparently resided at this
rather amazing house from the late fifteenth century, with the
exception of about 150 years, until the present day. Traquair is one of
the finest museums of the history of the area, as also of many members
of Scottish royalty and the great families. It possesses many rare and
very beautiful as well as intensely interesting articles and ancient
documents. There cannot be many people who will fail to find
something of interest and enjoyment in this great and ancient Scottish
home which is open to the public during the summer months. It was
at Traquair that the great city of Glasgow received its initial start, for
it was at Traquair that King William the Lion in 1175 granted a charter
to Bishop Jocelyn to found a Bishop's Burgh on the banks of a stream
known as the Molendinar, with the right to hold a market on
Thursdays. That small village has grown into the largest city in
Scotland, Glasgow. A copy of this charter can be seen at Traquair.
The great Bear Gates were closed on the failure of the Jacobites,
never to be opened until a Stuart is again on the throne.

Black Dwarf

A secondary road runs south from Peebles down the Manor Valley
to Manor Head, the end of the road, but from where a right of way
traverses the hills to St. Mary's Loch in Selkirkshire. The run to Manor
Head is one of the quietest and most pleasant. Kirkton Manor Kirk
and the grave of Scott's Black Dwarf should be seen, as well as the
Dwarf's cottage a little farther on, on the left-hand side of the road.
Note the ruins on Castle Hill above the Manor Water and the superb
scenery of hill and dale. Also note the Manor Sware and the bridge
over the Manor Water just before its junction with the Tweed. On the
return journey turn right at Kirkton and return by Cademuir. The Manor
Water and surrounding countryside is fine walking country.

Neidpath Castle

A mile west of Peebles is Neidpath Castle, one of the few old
Border towers that remain in good order. When this remarkable old
Castle was built seems to be lost in the long ago—it was in existence
in 1310 and was known as the Castle of Peebles. It is six storeys high
and is worth a visit. The views of this magnificent and heavily wooded
reach of the Tweed are really beautiful. It is open to the public and
there is a small car-park. Westwards from the Castle the road follows
the Tweed for a short distance and then the Lyne Water, both very
beautiful valleys. Where the Tarth Water and the Lyne Water join
forces high up on the hill there stands Drochil Castle, now in partial
ruins although it is said that it was never completed; it makes a fine
picture in scenery that is both varied and beautiful. It has been taken
over by the National Trust for Scotland and is in a very dangerous state.

Whipman Play

If one turns right at Drochil Castle the road leads through Romano
Bridge and several bonny villages to the A701 going northwards to
Edinburgh. By turning left at Drochil Castle wooded country of very
exceptional beauty will be traversed as the road winds between the
steep and rounded hills to the A701, which it is advisable to cross
and continue by the side road through this peaceful and delightful
land to the A702, again going northwards along the east side of the
Pentland Hills to Edinburgh. This route takes one through the
lovely little village of West Linton, the scene of the Whipman Play
which originated in 1803.

Neidpath Castle

Dawyck House

Following the Tweed Valley south-westwards from Peebles is probably one of the finest lowland runs with high hills on both sides, and the road closely follows the Tweed to its source at the Devil's Beef Tub. Turn left at Lyne Church and follow the Tweed and the road to Stobo Kirk, where a stop should be made. It is one of the very few Norman parish churches in Scotland, and it was dedicated to St. Mungo. Much rebuilding has been done but a lot of original work remains; this is one of the very rare little village churches that possess a well-known and interesting history. Dawyck House and gardens are the next point of interest, although every yard of the countryside holds both beauty and interest. These gardens are famous for their varieties of trees and the tremendous show of daffodils; they are open to the public at certain times. Shortly the tiny but superbly beautiful hamlet of Drumelzier appears hidden among the Tweedside trees. High above and completing a glorious picture are the ruins of Finnis Castle. Shortly after Drumelzier the A701 is reached. Turn right here for the lovely villages of Broughton and Skirling, where many of the gardens have painted token-poles, and so very shortly into Biggar in Lanarkshire.

Devil's Beef Tub

However, if on reaching the A701 the motorist turns left or south he can follow this very good road along the very banks of the Tweed through beautiful Tweedsmuir, with the glorious open hills on either hand all the way to the source of this great river at the Devil's Beef Tub. This is one of the finest runs in the south of Scotland. Right on the southern boundary of Peeblesshire and five miles north of Moffat, just where the road twists a little to the right with a high cliff on the left and room for parking, leave the car and look northwards and steeply downhill to a bowl in the hills with but one outlet. This is the Devil's Beef Tub, which came by its name when, many, many years ago the Marquis of Annandale was chief of the Johnson gang, who were noted cattle-rustlers; the stolen cattle were held here until it was safe to dispose of them. It was known as the Marquis of Annandale's Beef Tub until the title died.

Delightful Countryside

Peeblesshire is a county of hills and valleys, a delightful country of wide open spaces with only two towns of any size at all, Peebles and Innerleithen. For the caravanner, the camper and the hill-walker this is some of the finest country there is. For those who prefer to stay in a comfortable hotel and see the country by day-trips, then Peebles, Innerleithen and the wide hills and valleys should supply all that can be required.

Section 3

GLASGOW

Population: 1,800,000.
Early Closing Day: Tuesday or Saturday. Most shops in City centre are open six days.
Tourist Information Centre: George Square.
Museums: Art Gallery and Museum, Kelvingrove Park; Camphill Museum, Queen's Park; Museum of Transport, Albert Drive; Old Glasgow Museum, Glasgow Green; Pollock House, Pollock Park; Tollcross Museum, Tollcross Park.

FIRST IMPRESSIONS ARE LIABLE to remain permanently with us, therefore it is important that a great city, a great seaport and the capital of the west of Scotland should be first seen to the best advantage. Here the traveller by sea has the advantage, for the journey up the Firth of Clyde passes the small but inspiring Ailsa Craig, between the beautiful Isle of Arran and the mainland, into the narrowing neck of the Firth between the islands of Bute and Great Cumbrae; then around the most beautiful stretch of this outstanding coastline to Gourock, Greenock, and the busy River Clyde, leading to the docks from which ships sail to all ports of the world; it is inspiring and impressionable. While the southern bank of the river gets more and more crowded the northern bank still retains much of the loveliness for which the riverside of Dumbartonshire is famous. The River Clyde made Glasgow and the River is still the finest entrance.

Origins

The beginnings of Glasgow were very tiny indeed. In 1175 there was no vestige of the great city of today, for it was in that year that King William the Lion granted a charter to Bishop Jocelyn to found a Bishop's Burg on the Molendiner, with the right to hold a market on Thursdays. Thus started this great seaport and manufacturing city. Glasgow grew as did other places. Shipbuilding from the earliest days, trade by sea with other lands, agriculture and the earliest beginnings of manufacturing; all these used the River Clyde as an inlet and an outlet, and also, on its higher reaches, as a source of power.

After the Romans

The Romans were here, notwithstanding several intervals, for three hundred years, and left an indelible mark on the life and future of Scotland. During the thousand years after the Romans left these shores, much, but not all, of their crafts and skills were forgotten or destroyed. However, nothing is ever entirely forgotten, no good work is ever entirely discarded, and so the Romans must be counted among the first great teachers of civilisation to the Scots. The Vikings, the Saxons and many others, including the English, played their part for good or ill. Out of this thousand years of turmoil, until the fifteenth century, there began to emerge a nation with the skills and crafts that have since been carried by Scotsmen all over the world, skills and crafts that have developed a nation of world-wide renown, particularly in a few specialised crafts at which the Scots excel. And with the nation Glasgow grew and prospered. In many of the crafts and skills

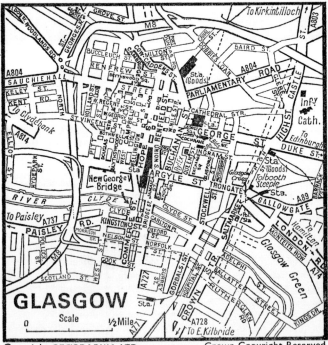

GLASGOW

0 Scale ½ Mile

of the early days Glasgow led the nation finally to become, in the twentieth century, one of the great manufacturing cities of the world, a famous and renowned shipbuilding centre, a cultural and academic centre of no mean repute and one of the great seaports of the world.

Britain's Third Port

There are one or two points of contemporary interest worth mentioning. Glasgow is bigger by far than the three other big cities of Scotland, Edinburgh, Aberdeen and Dundee; Glasgow can contain all three with room to spare. There are more Gaelic-speaking people in Glasgow than in any other city in the world and it is probably the most cosmopolitan. Glasgow is Britain's third port and one of the largest shipbuilding centres.

PAISLEY

Population: 97,000.
Early Closing Day: Tuesday.
Market Day: Monday.

FOR AN INDUSTRIAL BURGH the size of Paisley there is more beauty, more of nature's gifts and many more pleasant places preserved than one would expect. Particularly rich in parks and open spaces, astride the White Cart River and only three miles from the Clyde where it begins to lose a little of its industrial spoliation, Paisley has indeed done well to retain so much of what is natural and beautiful. It is five miles south-west of Glasgow. Immediately south of Paisley are the Brownside and Gleniffer Braes and two lochs. On the west, and actually within the town, is a reservoir with the ruins of a castle on an island.

The Hammils

Within the town there is much to see. Just above the Abbey Bridge the river forms an imposing waterfall called The Hammils. This is particularly fine when the river is in spate. Paisley was the county town of Renfrewshire and dates back to the days before written history; it is also the largest Burgh in Scotland.

Paisley Abbey

Paisley Abbey was founded in 1163 on the banks of the River Cart as a monastery for the monks of the Cluniac Order; in 1245 it was raised to the rank of Abbey. In 1307 it was completely destroyed by

the English and absolutely nothing of the original building remains.
During the reign of the Stewarts it was rebuilt in a much grander form
on the scale of a cathedral. During the centuries much damage has
been done but care and continual restoration has preserved an Abbey
of great beauty and distinction. Among the other places that should
be seen are the Town Hall in the tree-studded gardens; the Fountain
Gardens with a statue of Robert Burns; the Museum and Art Gallery;
the Thomas Coats Memorial Church (Baptist), which is claimed to be
the finest nonconformist church in Europe. The wood, marble and
stone carvings should not be missed. The Coats Observatory, the
Grammar School founded in 1576 and many other beautiful or
interesting places are worth a visit.

Paisley Weaving

Industrially Paisley owes its importance in the past to weaving, and
today, to thread, the millions of miles of thread of many kinds that
have been spun here. As far back as 1695 weaving was a popular
trade, producing many articles from wool, linen, cotton and mixed
materials. In time silk weaving, the Paisley Shawl, tapestries, and all
the changing fashions of the nineteenth century made Paisley the most
famous weaving town in Great Britain. By the end of last century this
famous but continually changing trade had come to an end, and was
quickly replaced by the manufacture of thread. From one mill alone
eighty million miles of cotton thread are turned out every year. Many
other industries have invaded Paisley but thread-making remains the
greatest.

EAST KILBRIDE

Population: 66,000.
Early Closing Day: Wednesday or Saturday.

THE BURGH OF EAST KILBRIDE, eight miles south-east of Glasgow,
is known to have been in existence before the Romans arrived and
when this part of Lanarkshire was a morass. In the late eighteenth
century there were less than 3,000 inhabitants, although shoe-making
and muslin weaving were important local industries. Coal-mining was a
short-lived industry for the seams were thin and of poor quality. It is
a remarkable fact that not until 1946, when the village was of a
purely agricultural type with a population of only 2,400, did any
growth take place. It was in 1947 that the new town of East Kilbride
came into being by a Designation Order signed on 6 May, 1947, and
was thus the first New Town in Scotland. In the last quarter of a

century it has grown industrially to its present population of nearly 50,000. It is in the widest possible sense that engineering may be said to represent the greatest portion of the industrial life of the town today. Clothing, manufacturing and many smaller and very diverse industries occupy an important position in this largely engineering town.

Mains Castle

The crumbling ruins of Mains Castle, of sixteenth-century origin and built on the site of an earlier tower, is the oldest surviving building. Another house of note, Torrance House, of seventeenth-century origin, stands in 300 acres of very beautiful grounds along the banks of the Calder Water. This is a most impressive battlemented house, once the home of the Stuarts, and is being converted into a hotel, while the large grounds will become a sports centre with artificial ski-slope.

Right in the centre of the old town is the Old Parish Church, which stands on the site of the very first church in East Kilbride. It was rebuilt in 1774 and its outstanding feature is the open Scots belfry, similar to the Glasgow Tolbooth.

Shopping Precinct

The Town Centre Shopping Precinct certainly deserves mention. It occupies 44 acres and is largely traffic-free. Flower-beds, an unusual circular restaurant, fountains and the noted Olympic Ballroom are only a few of the unusual features of this very modern centre. The chief pride of East Kilbride is the swimming-pool. It was opened in 1968 and among the many luxurious features are the Turkish baths, a games room, a gallery for 600 spectators, a spacious foyer and a laundry. It is, in addition, the first full Olympic length bath in Scotland and has a special learners' pool.

HAMILTON

Population: 48,000.
Early Closing Day: Wednesday.
Market Days: Monday, Wednesday.

THE BURGH OF HAMILTON was at one time an important coal-mining area, but this has now given place to a host of new industries which include electronics, printing, aluminium refining and many others. The County Council of Lanarkshire have most of their offices and services concentrated in Hamilton. It has a reputation as one of the best shopping centres in this very densely populated district of

Southern Scotland. To the south there is open farmland and along the banks of the Clyde there are many delightful spots along the southern reaches of the river. Northwards towards Glasgow the Clyde gets more industrialised.

BLANTYRE

Population: 17,757.
Early Closing Day: Wednesday.

BLANTYRE, BIRTHPLACE OF DAVID LIVINGSTONE, the great explorer and missionary, is situated on the A776 Road, just west of the Hamilton-Rutherglen road. Livingstone, one of five children, was born in 1813, two years before Waterloo and his father worked selling tea but was unable to earn much money. Nevertheless the family was very respectable, fiercely religious and the children were taught to respect learning. David especially was a natural scholar, though all the children were encouraged to read good books.

Young Scholar

At the age of ten, Livingstone was put to work in the Dale Mills, near his home, and it was an early sign of his remarkable character that after a long day in the mill, often not finishing till ten at night, the boy would pore over a Latin grammar book by candlelight. His aim was to master enough Latin to get himself a place in college on a scholarship. Amazingly, considering the odds against him, he won a place at Anderson's College in Glasgow where he studied medicine, theology and Greek. In 1838 he was accepted by the London Missionary Society and two years later took his final medical degree. Then he began his extraordinary career as a missionary and doctor, traveller and explorer in what was then called 'Darkest Africa'.

Victoria Falls

In the course of his wanderings through the 'dark' Continent he discovered the Victoria Falls and became involved with Sir Richard Burton's efforts to find the source of the River Nile. He married the daughter of a fellow missionary, but she and their children were obliged to leave Africa due to ill-health. Livingstone went on with his labours, making only rare visits to London. In 1862 Mrs. Livingstone died and though this was a terrible blow Livingstone continued his work which now involved the exposure of the slave trade which was still going on in Africa.

Stanley

For some time he was thought to be 'lost' or dead, but the famous expedition of the American journalist H. M. Stanley resulted in the discovery of the great doctor and missionary at Ujiji in 1871. It is now a household story how Stanley greeted the frail-looking white doctor with the memorable words—'Dr. Livingstone, I presume'. Stanley spent some time with Livingstone and his African staff and fellow-workers, but only two years later, when he was sixty, this amazing child of the Regency who had lived to become the pillar of Victorian missionary fervour died, worn out by his efforts. He was buried in Westminster Abbey in 1874.

National Memorial

The house in Shuttle Row, where David Livingstone was born is now part of the Scottish National Memorial to him—the finest of its kind in the world. The cottage and its contents reflect a picture of the socio-economic times in which Livingstone grew up and in addition there is a remarkable collection of things connected with his later life, including maps, and personal relics. The ruins of Dales Mills are still visible near the cottage, but there is a reconstructed working model of the mill in its heyday, along with the photographs and documents in the museum collection.

The spacious grounds outside contain fine tableaux, models of African kraals and, in addition, plenty of attractions for children as well as refreshment facilities. There are special picnic spots too which help to make the Livingstone Memorial an excellent place for a family excursion.

MOTHERWELL AND WISHAW

Population: 77,000.
Early Closing Day: Wednesday or Saturday.

IN THE DIM AND DISTANT PAST Motherwell and Wishaw were two rural villages twelve miles south-east of Glasgow. In fact it was not until the nineteenth century that any great change occurred. Then coal mined at Wishaw served to fire the furnaces at Motherwell and their industrial future was assured. Now they are almost part of that huge industrial area that very nearly links Glasgow and Edinburgh, though still a Burgh in Lanarkshire. A few spots remain to remind us of the more spacious and less noisy days of not so long ago. Dalzell House is on the site of the ancient church of the same name; Dalziel or Dall Zell is ancient Scots for "I Dare". The name Motherwell is derived from a well dedicated to the Virgin Mary, and the original cope stone of this well is still in its original position, so that those of an antiquarian turn of mind may see the Lady Well from which the village took its name, probably in the eleventh century. The name Wishaw has had several changes but originated as Waygateshaw, meaning the gate in a wood. Today Motherwell and Wishaw are hives of industry, very largely engineering in its many forms. Even as near Glasgow as this, about twelve miles, the Clyde still has some very beautiful reaches where the visitor can forget the noise and bustle of the industrial burghs for a few hours.

LARKHALL

Population: 34,471.
Early Closing Day: Wednesday.

LARKHALL, A MAINLY INDUSTRIAL TOWN, is delightfully tucked away between the beautiful River Avon and Clydesdale, where that great river commences to leave the industrial surroundings of the huge Glasgow area and is five miles south-east of Hamilton. The most outstanding features of Larkhall are the Morgan Glen, described as the finest natural park in the west of Scotland, and the seventeenth-century village of Millheugh. A footpath encircles the village and the Glen, passing under the highest railway viaduct in Scotland to the Linn and some really glorious scenery. Farther down the Avon, close to Hamilton, are the ruins of Cadzow Castle.

Larkie Fair

Opposite Larkhall on the banks of the Clyde is the village of Dalserf, where the ancient Castle of Tillietudlem is mentioned by Sir Walter Scott in *Old Mortality*. This reach of the Clyde is particularly beautiful and the village of Dalserf sets off the natural scenery to perfection. Once a large coal-mining area, Larkhall changed its industrial pattern to include many and varied industries. This whole district along the Clyde is a quite famous tomato- and fruit-growing area. It was not until the reign of George II that Larkhall relinquished its village status —its ancient name was Laverockha'. The Larkie Fair, which was the hiring time for farm-workers, is still held on the last Friday of June. The partly riverside road from Dalserf to Hamilton is much to be preferred to the road from Larkhall. For the exploring motorist there are numerous tiny lanes leading down to the Avon and the Clyde, where peace and lovely scenery may be enjoyed within a few miles of Glasgow.

CARLUKE

Population: 12,000.
Early Closing Day: Wednesday. All day on the third Wednesday of every month.

CARLUKE, LIKE OTHER PLACES in the district, was once a mining village three miles south-east of Wishaw; now, in the town itself are light engineering works. The area is rural and famed for its fruit and vegetable market-gardens. The town itself is extremely pleasant, the market being a well-laid-out park with the War Memorial and flower-beds. The Cross is the centre of the town and merely the intersection of five roads.

Covenanters' Memorial

Opposite the Town Hall is the Tower of the old Parish Church, which was rebuilt on its present site in 1799, and alongside is the old burial ground. Not far away, on The Moor, is the Covenanters' Memorial; as with so many parts of South Scotland the Covenanters of this area played a noble and important part in securing freedom of religious worship.

Tower of Hallbar

There are many quiet side roads leading down to the lovely banks of the Clyde, where riverside walks of great beauty abound. Just south of Carluke is the village of Braidwood, with a delightful loch partly surrounded by woods, and a little nearer the Clyde is the Tower of Hallbar. This ancient Border pele is in remarkably good order for a building reputed to date from the twelfth century. It is in a rather difficult situation to approach but is very well worth a visit. Carluke is a small town in a beautiful countryside, with a wealth of parks and open spaces of more than usual attractiveness.

RENFREW

Population: 18,964.
Early Closing Day: Wednesday.

RENFREW IS A ROYAL BURGH in the small but extremely varied and healthy Renfrewshire. It is situated on the south bank of the River Clyde just where the River Cart joins it, and is only six miles west of Glasgow. A modern industrial town on the verge of some of the finest river and moorland scenery in Southern Scotland, it has a long and proud history, a busy industrial present and a future that holds out hopes of a Burgh far removed in appearance and standards from the industrial poverty and squalor of the Victorian era and the industrial revolution.

Constant Warfare

The Romans had a camp or fort here and later it was part of the Kingdom of Strathclyde. The history of Renfrew was much like that of any other Scottish riverside town—constant warfare and bloodshed, for the Vikings attacked the west coast as well as the east. In addition to attacks from outside, internal strife, due largely to the age-old clan system, kept Scotland in a continual state of warfare until the Union of the Crowns of Scotland and England in 1603. The Burgh is thought to have originated in the early twelfth century.

Prince of Wales

Renfrew Castle, which stood on Castle Hill between the town and the river, has long since completely disappeared, apart from some traces of the moat. It was here that in 1370 Robert II, the first Stewart King of Scotland, was born. In 1396 Robert III created Renfrew a Royal Burgh and in 1404 the Burgh bestowed the title Baron Renfrew on the heir-apparent to the Scottish throne, and this title is still held by the Prince of Wales. The prosperity of Renfrew saw many ups and downs from the fourteenth century to the nineteenth, since when, apart from the 1930's, it has continued to grow. At one time it was the Clyde's principal port, largely during the seventeenth century. To the west is Abbotsinch Airport, which serves Glasgow. Today its manufactures cover a very wide range which include tyres, cables, refined oils and the largest boiler works in Great Britain.

Johnstone

Population: 25,000.
Early Closing Day: Tuesday.

The Burgh of Johnstone stands on the banks of the Black Cart Water which flows into the Clyde. Johnstone is still just within the huge industrial area of Glasgow. It is four miles south-west of Paisley. Unlike most towns of any age at all, Johnstone was started as a planned town in 1780 by one George Houston, in time for the tremendous boost of the industrial revolution. The original planning, parallel streets and squares survive to this day. The river supplied the power for the early industries before the age of steam. Johnstone lies just west of Paisley and south of that great Abbey town lies another interesting industrial town with a population of 16,000. Here, at Barrhead, as in

Johnstone, the first house was built in the middle of the eighteenth century. Weaving was the first village industry, followed by bleaching on the discovery that the River Levern was peculiarly fitted for this process. Cotton spinning followed and before long this quiet village on the northern edge of the moors became a busy town, and then a Burgh in 1894. Many of the heights surrounding Barrhead, chiefly to the west, afford some splendid views. Killoch Glen is a beautiful wooded Glen that comes as a surprise in an otherwise industrial area and should not be missed.

PORT GLASGOW

Population: 22,633.
Early Closing Day: Wednesday.
Tourist Information Office: Town Clerk, Town Buildings.

PORT GLASGOW IS ANOTHER OF the Clydeside towns that had a late start in life but grew with speed and energy. It is less than three hundred years old. In the seventeenth century some Glasgow merchants were much troubled by the shallow water of the river, which prevented larger vessels sailing right into Glasgow's centre for discharge and loading of cargo. These enterprising men picked a deep-water spot next to Newark Castle and made a fresh deep-water port. The harbours were constructed in 1688, and immediately Port Glasgow started on the road to prosperity. Many different cargoes were imported and fish was exported. When the steam age arrived shipbuilding began, achieved a world-wide reputation and still holds it. In 1812 Port Glasgow inaugurated the first steamship service in Great Britain between Port Glasgow, Greenock and Helensburgh. The first steamship to be built on the Clyde was the *Charlotte Dundas,* in 1801.

Westwards from the centre of Port Glasgow all is industrial and dockside noise, but eastwards the prospect becomes almost rural as far as Clydebank. Behind the town and along the Clyde eastwards the ground rises steeply, affording some magnificent scenery of far-away hills in all directions, and of this famous river with its continuous stream of shipping. Two miles east of the town and right on the riverside is the National Trust of Scotland property included in Parklea Recreation Ground. This is a particularly beautiful spot with magnificent views of the estuary.

Newark Castle
The oldest building is Newark Castle, of fifteenth century date and under the care of the Dept. of Environment and of course open to the

public; it stands on a small headland not far from the town centre. The Parish Church was built in 1823 but Newark Church is some fifty years older. Naturally in a town of this age there are few old and interesting buildings, but Port Glasgow can offer the visitor some grander scenery, from very close by, than almost any other industrial town. The riverside westwards from Port Glasgow assumes no particular interest or beauty until Greenock is reached.

LANARK

Population: 8,500.
Early Closing Day: Thursday. All day on second Thursday of each month.
Market Day: Monday.

LANARK HAS BEEN A Royal Burgh since 1140, when King David conferred this honour on the then tiny but important town. As early as 978 a parliament was held here, and later Kings of Scotland stayed here at the Castle that stood on the small hillock at the foot of Castlegate, and very close to the Clyde.

St. Kentigern

St. Kentigern's Church and the Old Kirkyard are the oldest buildings remaining. There is not a great deal left of what was, as long ago as the twelfth century, the Parish Church. But that little is singularly beautiful, and in conjunction with the very ancient Kirkyard is extremely moving. The Monks of Dryburgh held St. Kentigern from about 1150 until the Restoration. Two men of very different characters lie within the south aisle: Irvine of Bonshaw, an entirely ruthless persecutor of the Covenanters, and William Hervi, who was executed at Lanark Cross in 1682 for his beliefs and the Reformation.

Grammar School

The Parish Church of St. Nicholas is an entirely typical Scottish Kirk of the eighteenth century. The stained-glass windows are of a very high order, while the very extensive roof is supported by immense and massive beams. Unlike most Kirks of this period, the congregation sit in front of the minister, normally they sit on three sides of the pulpit. The tower, with a very fine statue of Wallace, makes an imposing frontage and faces the main shopping street. In the tower is the bell, which is believed to be 800 years old although recast three times since, which rings out the toll at strictly observed times. There are several eighteenth-century buildings close to St. Nicholas. Hyndford House, dated 1773, is a very fine example of a Scottish nobleman's house of that period. The Grammar School has a history which dates from 1183 and was founded by the Monks of Dryburgh Abbey.

Historic Interest

New Lanark, only recently incorporated into the Burgh, was founded in the 1780s by David Dale and Richard Arkwright as the centre of a new venture in cotton-spinning. Dale's son-in-law, Robert Owen, who took control in 1800, found that the living conditions of the workers were absolutely frightful. Education and sanitation were almost non-existent, while crime and vice were rampant. He set about improving their lot in many ways and was responsible for the first infant school in Great Britain. The mills were forced to close in 1968 but the New Lanark Association Ltd. is having a lot of success in preserving this village, which is of very considerable social and historic interest.

Surroundings

Today Lanark is a clean and tidy town within an hour's drive of some of the most spectacular country in Southern Scotland. North-westwards along the Clyde Valley there are many small towns and villages between Lanark and Hamilton—some have been mentioned, but space does not permit of the mention of every one in such a closely populated area. However, the motorist with an exploring turn of mind will find much that is both beautiful and interesting that has not been recorded here.

White Craws

Some seven miles east of Lanark is the ancient village of Carnwath, a little more than a mile north of a sharp bend in the Clyde. This was the scene of the famous "Carnwath Mill" song, "We're no awa' tae bide awa'". It is attributed to Archie Nimmo, a great Clydesdale man who also wrote about the "White Craws that flee backwards to keep the stour oot their een". Carnwath men are still known as White Craws. Actually Carnwath dates back to at least 1116. A mile north of the railway station are the ruins of Couthally Castle, the ancient home of the Fighting Somervilles. Later they moved to the Double Tower and then to Carnwath House, which still stands opposite the Parish Church. Of this fifteenth-century church St. Mary's Aisle is all that is left of the original, the rest is rebuilt. Nearby and south of Clydesdale Forest are the Red and White Lochs. This is a very beautiful little village without even one factory chimney and well screened by trees.

E

Railway Town

About two miles west of Carnwath is another picture-book village that carries the older folks straight back to the quiet days of horses: Carstairs, with its village green encircled by trees, with the War Memorial facing the Parish Church, inside which there is a lot of interest and beauty. Between these two delightful spots and a little to the south is Carstairs Junction, a purely railway town that is the junction of the routes to Edinburgh and Glasgow of the former Caledonian Railway, the three points of the triangle junction being called Carstairs Junction to the west, Dolphinton Junction to the north-east and the oddly named Strawfrank Junction to the south-east.

Rocky Burns

North of Lanark on the A706 is the village of Forth. It stands at little less than 1,000 feet above sea-level on the western side of the Pentland Hills, where moorland and rocky burns are the outstanding features. Once almost entirely a coal-mining village with a character of its own, the large council estates have entirely destroyed that character, however, to the lover of the hills and wide open moorlands the country around is superb; the Mouse Water and the Abbey Burn are two delightful streams.

Lovely Countryside

West of Lanark and south of Larkhall, in that lovely countryside that borders the rich Clyde Valley, there are one or two places of interest, although the whole countryside is green and beautiful though dotted here and there with the outlying extensions of the nearby industry so close to the north. For all its industrial outliers, in spite of the nearness of the big industrial towns and in spite of the multiplicity of roads, the Clyde Valley, if one takes the trouble to explore it, is as beautiful and green as any in Southern Scotland, but it is naturally interspersed with towns and villages that are not as picturesque.

Stonehouse

Population: 5,000.
Early Closing Day: Wednesday.

The village of Stonehouse is very pleasantly situated in rich farmland yet close to the wide open moors. The most outstanding feature of Stonehouse is the peace that pervades the atmosphere. The Parish Church was dedicated to St. Ninian, of the ninth century. Stonehouse is alongside the River Avon and the bridge, undated, is well worthy of inspection. During the centuries of Border warfare and internal strife this was the country of the House of Douglas, at one time the most powerful family in Scotland. At least one covenanter from this lovely little village, Patrick Hamilton, was burned at the stake.

Strathaven

Population: 6,000.
Early Closing Day: Wednesday.

Strathaven, in the Valley of the River Avon and sheltered by the Ayrshire hills, enjoys a temperate healthy climate. Being on the A71 a good route from Glasgow or Edinburgh, it receives a lot of week-end visitors. Close to the Valley of the Clyde and closer still to the moors which stretch for many miles southwards, it offers the walker many alternative routes in different types of country. Westwards into the Ayrshire hills the motorist can enjoy quiet roads and restful driving. Southwards he must proceed by Lesmahagow to the east or Muirkirk to the west, for no motor roads travel over the vast moorlands to the south-east of Strathaven.

Ducal Gift

The Castle of Strathaven, built in the early fourteenth century, has been gifted by the Duke of Hamilton to the town of Strathaven, and the grounds in which it stands have been restored by the authorities so that the people of this delightful little town have a park of historic interest and great beauty. There are three other parks, the George Allan, the John Hastie and the Allison Green. As far back as the fifteenth century weaving was a considerable industry here, and even as late as the early nineteenth century there were 400 weavers. By 1930 only three of the old-time weavers were left. Today three silk mills have taken the place of the hand-looms, and the surrounding countryside supports a great and growing dairy industry. The monument to James Wilson should raise very serious thoughts among the workers of this affluent twentieth century; he was beheaded on Glasgow Green in 1802 for his leadership of the weavers' rising. Today this would be called a strike, not a rising, and the standard of living enjoyed by James Wilson was very near the lowest possible. St. Ninian's Churchyard and St. Osan's Well are within easy and comfortable walking distance, while a footpath leads to Spectacle E'e Falls from the neighbouring village of Sandford.

Glassford Castle

Two miles north of Strathaven on a side road is the little village of Glassford, which is well worth a visit. The ancient church and remains

of Glassford Castle should be seen. In this corner of Lanarkshire there
are many, many places of beauty and interest that have not been
mentioned—space simply does not allow the author to mention more
than the most important. Take a detailed Ordnance Survey Map and
go exploring.

BIGGAR

Population: 1,738.
Early Closing Day: Wednesday.
Market Day: Thursday.

BIGGAR IS A VERY SPACIOUS and extremely bright little town
with a sense of freedom about it. Although very close to the River
Clyde, the Biggar Water, on both sides of which the town is built,
actually flows eastwards to join the Tweed. Biggar is indeed in an enviable
position geographically. To the north are the Pentland Hills, with good
roads on either side leading to Edinburgh. On the west is the lower
Clyde and good roads to Glasgow. On the east is the green and
beautiful valley of the Tweed. Southwards, both east and west, are the
wide open hills, the moorlands from which both the Tweed and the
Clyde take their source. This is the country that the motorist can cross
by only two roads, the A701 and the A708, but over which the walker
is free to choose his route. If he is experienced he can enjoy some of
the finest walking terrain in Southern Scotland; if he is a learner let
him beware, for these hills are wide, with few tracks.

Cadger's Bridge

In Biggar town there are a number of interesting points. Approaching
from the west the narrow but most attractive Cadger's Bridge will be
seen on the left-hand side of the road; tradition tells that the great
Wallace crossed this bridge in 1297 disguised as a hawker, or
"Cadger", hence the name. The sixteenth-century Church of St. Mary,
beautifully restored, is one of the last pre-Reformation churches in
Scotland. Within its framework are the remains of the twelfth-century
church of St. Nicholas. This beautifully restored church is the
pride of Biggar and the most exquisite building in the town. Within
the church are many things of interest; a list of ministers since
1164, a stool of repentance of 1694, communion cups of silver made
in 1650 and an old cannon from Boghall Castle.

Boghall Castle

The very few remaining ruins of Boghall Castle can be approached
by a footpath; it was once a large and powerful castle with great

natural defences in the morass surrounding it. It has associations with Mary Queen of Scots and was the seat of the Fleming family. The ruins are now in the care of the Biggar town council. In mid-summer the ceremony of the crowning of the Fleming Queen is celebrated ; this delightful day out commemorates Mary Fleming, who was discovered by Mary Queen of Scots at Boghall Castle, and became one of the four "Queen's Maries".

Viewpoint

To the west the whole area is dominated by the "Hill of Fire", Tinto Hill, from the summit of which, on a clear day, eighteen shires and the mountains of Cumberland are said to be visible. The best route to the summit is a footpath from a point close to the village of Thankerton, about four or five miles west of Biggar. The great hole on the summit of Tinto is known as "Wallace's Thumb-Mark". A little north of Thankerton is the old Border tower of Covington, which is well worthy of a visit from those who are interested in ancient architecture. On the Lanark road, some three to four miles from Biggar, is Symington, an old-world village with the Kirk as the centre and the houses around it ; the most interesting feature is the Kirk watch-house, a relic of body-snatching days, the earliest days of medical science.

Culter Water

From Biggar the A702 strikes southwards alongside the Clyde and into the heart of the Lowther Hills. Three miles south of Biggar turn left or east into the village of Culter, on the Culter Water, with the white Parish Church founded by the Monks of Kelso Abbey in 1170. Then continue up the hill southwards to the magnificent views from the 2,000-foot hills. Southwards from this road end are hills and lochs, wild and glorious country for the walker with, here and there, side tracks that will tempt the adventurous motorist.

Castle Crawford

Still sticking to the A702, Lamington is reached. This is one of the loveliest and most tree-shaded villages in Lanarkshire. In the northern wall of the very beautiful church is a Norman arch, survivor of a more ancient church. Now the road continues southwards right alongside the Clyde with some delightful scenery, of the Lowther hills on the east and the Clyde on the immediate west. Just across the river is the A73, which passes through the plain little village of Roberton to join the A74 at Abington, one of the busiest road junctions in Southern Scotland. The village itself, just to the east of the main highway, is tree-covered and wholly delightful. Continuing southwards along the A74, which winds alongside the ever narrowing Clyde, the delightful little village of Crawford is passed unless one turns left into the tree-shaded old village to join the main road a mile farther on. In the triangle formed by the Clyde and the Camp Burn, on a small hill-top, are the remains of Castle Crawford, only half a mile from the village.

Source of The Clyde

Three miles south of Crawford the highway crosses the Clyde to the east bank, while the triangle formed by the Elvan Water and the Clyde is occupied by the very scattered village of Elvanfoot, where Glengeith Farm has strong covenanter connections. There is no inn at Elvanfoot, so visitors and locals make the extremely beautiful five-mile trip over the hills to Leadhills, almost due west. Here at what is in reality the source of the Clyde, for many smaller streams join near Elvanfoot to form that great river, the A74 curves eastwards to follow the Clyde Burn to the Dumfries county boundary near the Devil's Beef Tub.

Daer Reservoir

The most southern point of Lanarkshire is Gana Hill (2,191 feet), but no roads approach within some miles of it. The western border of Lanarkshire can only be followed, in the county itself by a walker. However, several side roads leave the A74 to travel south and west into Dumfriesshire and Ayrshire. The first of these quiet side roads leaves Elvanfoot and travels southwards; this is the A702, through spectacular scenery and magnificent hills, following the Potrail Water to the county boundary at the watershed, the highest points of the hills, about 1,900 feet, and continues to Nithsdale. Three miles south of Elvanfoot a narrow road takes off on the left or east and threads its way along the Daer Water to the Daer Reservoir, and right along the western bank to the shepherd's cottage at Kirkhope. This is as far as any ordinary motorist would wish to go, however, there is a rough track excellent for walkers, which splits up into several footpaths. The road from

Wemyss Bay

Elvanfoot to Leadhills is another spectacular run and crosses the county boundary into Dumfriesshire at 1,600 feet. Leadhills and the surrounding countryside was, in the not so long ago, mining country, lead being one of the minerals obtained. Today that is all dead but the residue and some of the spoil-heaps and workings are beginning to blend in with nature and do not spoil the countryside as one might expect. Northwards from Leadhills a glorious run takes the motorist to Abington in about six or seven miles. And all around, without a break, are the hills, the walkers' paradise, with many a little-known glen and many a burn that has seldom seen a human.

Castle Dangerous

The A74 leaves Abington north-westwards for Glasgow. Three miles from Abington a narrow road takes off to the south-west for Sanquhar in Dumfriesshire. At the village of Crawfordjohn a side road takes off to the Leadhills—Abington road, and shortly another of these lanes goes northwards, otherwise there is nothing to disturb the everlasting peace of the hills; the highest on the east while to the west the heights slope gently away to the lower hills and finally the plains of Ayrshire. When the A74 reaches the glorious wooded and loch-studded valley of the Douglas Water, the motorist will want to stay awhile and finally turn west along the A70, while the A74 draws nearer and nearer to the thickly populated areas south and south-east of Glasgow. The village of Douglas, a little south of the junction of the two roads, is still the home of the Douglas family, who have been prominent in Scottish history at least since the time of Robert the Bruce. Their old home, Scott's "Castle Dangerous", is in ruins, but the very delightful grounds are open to the public. The Parish Church of St. Bride, which contains many relics of this famous family, should be visited. The clock in the church tower is reputed to have a been gift from Mary Queen of Scots.

Wedder Hill

This picturesque road which follows the Douglas Water along the narrow valley crosses the county boundary into Ayrshire alongside the Glenbuck Loch. North and south, east and west are the hills; the few roads are good ones and the caravanner should be attracted by the fine open country where individual sites are to be found at all sorts of unexpected spots, with the clear water of the hill burns at hand. South Lanarkshire is indeed a fine and open country. Wedder Hill (1,411 feet) is the south-west corner of Lanarkshire and, as with so much of this fine county, no roads approach this hill. There are, however, two more roads that most closely approach this part of the county, and both start from Strathaven. One runs along the northern bank of the Avon to cross the county boundary and continues to Kilmarnock; the

other follows the south bank of the Avon and, turning south, follows
the Glengavel Water to the Glengavel Reservoir.

GREENOCK
Population: 71,400.
Early Closing Day: Wednesday.

GREENOCK, POSSIBLY THE MOST FAMOUS port on the Clyde, is
the terminus for the larger ships that cannot venture up the
shallower waters of the Clyde. This factor was of far more importance
in years gone by, for the dredging and deepening of the river
upstream has somewhat diminished the advantage held for so long by
Greenock, for it is a moot point as to whether these famous harbours
stand on the river or on the Firth of Clyde. Greenock is a very ancient
town, once a tiny fishing village with the safest natural anchorage on
the Firth of Clyde or the river. In 1641 an act of the Scottish
Parliament ratified the Crown Charter granted in 1635 by Charles I,
by which the lands of Grenok-Shaw and the village of Grenok became
a Burgh of Barony. From that time onwards Greenock has grown to
become sixth among the cities and towns of Scotland.

Ship-building
In 1710 the first extensions to the natural harbour were completed
and, coinciding with the final union of Scotland and England, led to
an immediate and lasting improvement in worldwide trade. From time
immemorial a ship-building port, it has increased its capacity and
output until now ships built at Greenock are known all over the
world. One firm alone, and still building ships, started in 1711. The
first Greenock ship to cross the Atlantic did so in 1684. One ship of
the historic Darien Expedition was fitted out at Greenock.
   Among the other principal industries is sugar refining, sack making,
woollen manufacturing, rope making, chemical manufacturing,
electronic computers and a host of others ; but it is still as a deep-water
harbour and shipbuilding centre that Greenock is best known.

James Watt
In 1736 James Watt was born in Greenock and first conceived the
idea of using steam as a source of power. A handsome monument to
him stands in Dalrymple Street. Captain Kidd, the famous pirate who
was hanged in 1701, had connections with the town. Robert Burns's
Highland Mary died in Greenock and is remembered by a cairn in
Greenock cemetery.

Highland Mary

The figure of the frail Highland girl who loved Burns so desperately, flits wraith-like through the robust annals of Burns' short but prolific career. Their brief love, enforced parting, and her pathetic death, far from her Highland home and friends, plus the fact that she was carrying Burns' child when she became ill and died, evokes our sympathy and commiseration. But at least her poet-lover conferred immortality upon her with the verses he wrote about her, and especially in the "Ode to Mary in Heaven" which opens with an invocation to the morning star which heralded the anniversary of her death:

> Thou lingering star with lessening ray
> That lov'st to greet the early morn,
> Again thou usherest in the day,
> My Mary from my soul was torn.

Greenock today is very largely a pleasant, clean town with one outstanding feature that was put there by nature but which man has improved upon to such an extent that it is now one of the most pleasant places on the Clyde, the beautiful and handsome riverside drive from Greenock to its near neighbour Gourock; a pleasanter drive or walk it would be hard to find anywhere; especially so close to the tremendous industrial area of Greater Glasgow.

GOUROCK

Population: 11,250.
Early Closing Day: Wednesday.

THE BURGH OF GOUROCK is the first of the holiday resorts along the Firth of Clyde, but it was not until 1889 when the railway extended its line to Gourock that this Firth-side town really began to extend its facilities and natural beauties into a resort for the teeming population of Glasgow, and later still for the world at large. It has a delightful situation on the corner of the Firth and the river with some high and open country immediately behind it, offering walks and motor runs of spectacular beauty, and extensive views. It was in 1694 that the then fishing village of Gourock received its charter as a Burgh of Barony, and as late as 1881 the population was still only 3,300. More than three-quarters the development of Gourock has taken place in the last half-century. Today it is an important passenger port for trips to the Kyles of Bute, Rothesay, Arran, or along the Clyde and other nearby places. An outstanding landmark for ships entering the Clyde is Cloch Point Lighthouse, where visitors are shown over at the discretion of the keeper.

Yachting Centre

Immediately west of Gourock and beyond the point of Gourock Bay is Ashton, a famous centre for yachting with all the usual seaside holiday attractions. The walk along this part of the coast, as with the esplanade between Greenock and Gourock, is unsurpassed for its views of the Clyde, the Firth and the further views embracing the islands and the opposite hills of Dunbartonshire and Argyllshire. Only by climbing the hills inland can the picture be improved upon, and from some of the highest points the scene at times is beyond description.

Open Moorland

The County of Renfrew is a long narrow strip from south-east to north-west; at its longest point it is about forty miles and at its widest about twelve to fifteen. Most of this area of nearly 500 square miles is industrialised to a greater or lesser extent; a great deal of very beautiful country lies in between many of the industrial areas and almost the whole of the southern boundary with Ayrshire for a width of several miles consists of open moorland dotted with lochs and heights of up to 1,700 feet. North of Lochwinnoch almost to Greenock and Gourock and bounded on the west side by the coast is one area of open moorland, where the motor roads run only around the moors and at no point do they cross it. Farther east, south-east of the East Kilbride—Kilmarnock road, there is another similar area though a great deal smaller in extent. Throughout all this country, both industrial and open moorland, there are a lot of very beautiful and some interesting places that have not been mentioned so far. The following are some of the finest.

Auchenbothie Castle. At least thirteenth century and owned by Sir William Wallace. On the roadside close to Rosebank Reservoir on the B776, south-west of Johnstone.

Ballagiech Height, (1,084 feet), half a mile north of the Kilbride—Kilmarnock road and three miles south-west of Eaglesham; half mile climb on foot, magnificent views.

Barochan Cross, twelfth century, Dept. of Environment. On east side of road two miles north of Houston which is four miles north-west of Johnstone. Fourteenth-century Cross in Houston village.

Barr Castle, an old four-storey pele one mile south of Lochwinnoch on Kilbirnie road between road and Barr Loch.

Bishopton, between Glasgow and Port Glasgow, fine golf-course in very pleasant countryside.

Bridge of Weir, by the Gryfe Water. Lovely scenery, fishing. On road from Johnstone to Port Glasgow.

Corlic Hill above Greenock, wonderful views. Summit reached on foot from Old Largs Road.

Covenanters Hollow. A tiny grass-grown glen on the upper moorlands. Meeting place of Covenanters in seventeenth century. Fine scenery and views. Can be reached only on foot from Ladymuir Farm, which is one mile west of the Lochwinnoch—Kilmacolm road four to five miles north of Lochwinnoch.

Devol Glen, a wooded glen in the hills behind Port Glasgow and close to Harelaw Reservoir.

Eaglesham, a lovely village rebuilt in the eighteenth century, four miles south-west of East Kilbride. Turn north at Eaglesham over splendid scenes along the White Cart Water.

Elderslie, just south of the Paisley—Johnstone road. Reputed birthplace of Sir William Wallace, thirteenth century. There is a cross beside an old farmhouse, which is supposed to be the actual birthplace.

Gleniffer Braes. A fine upland piece of country with fine views. The B775 runs alongside, past a lovely waterfall, The Linn.

Hill of Stake, a lonely windswept hill (1,711 feet) on the Ayrshire boundary; one mile east is Misty Law (1,662 feet), fine walkers' country with extensive views.

Loch Thom. Good fishing on lofty moorland. Reached by the Old Largs Road.

Mearns Castle. Ruins of fifteenth-century stronghold. Close to Castle Farm, just north of the Mearns—Waterford road. Waterford is on the Glasgow—Eaglesham road.

Polnoon Castle of the fourteenth century. Open to the public. One mile south of Eaglesham turn left with main road, half-mile to Castle.

Stanley Castle, fifteenth century. On the edge of Stanley Reservoir which must once have been a natural loch. On the western outskirts of Paisley close to the B775.

Waterfoot. A delightful spot and favourite angling haunt at the junction of the Earn Water and White Cart Water. Two and a half miles north of Eaglesham.

West Ferry is a motorists' halt on the Clyde, opposite Dumbarton, and with some splendid views, a mile and a half east of Langbank.

On the west coast there are three little places that no visitor should miss. After leaving Gourock and Ashton, Lunderston Bay is rounded, and then comes the very lovely little village of Inverkip.

Beyond the site of Dunrod Castle is a fifteenth- or sixteenth-century bridge often referred to as a Roman bridge. Wemyss Bay—there was once a Castle of Wemyss—is the last place of interest before crossing the Ayrshire boundary.

AYR

Population: 50,000.
Early Closing Day: Wednesday.
Market Day: Tuesday.
Tourist Information Office: 30 Miller Road.

THIS VERY POPULAR HOLIDAY RESORT lies about half-way along the coast of Ayrshire. It was the County Town and has been a Royal Burgh since 1202. For the holidaymaker who is looking for golden sands, the promenade, play pools and parks for the youngsters, in fact for all those things that have come to be considered as part of the holiday by the seaside, then Ayr can hardly be bettered. It is a great shopping town with all the amenities that one could expect. For the more individualistic holidaymaker, the lover of the wild windswept coast, of the lochs and open moorlands, of the green and pleasant valleys and the wild forgotten hilltops. Ayr is a grand centre in which to replenish supplies for further exploration into the less-well-known country around.

The Auld Kirk

Within the town itself there are a number of things that most people would wish to see: old and beautiful relics of the past history of the town that now offers so much delight and pleasure. On the north side of High Street is the Kirk Port, a narrow entrance to the Auld Kirk or the New Church of St. John the Baptist. It was built in 1654. Behind the building of this church is an interesting bit of history. During the period of the Commonwealth, between 1649 and 1660, Cromwell's soldiers decided that Ayr should be fortified, the better to control south-west Scotland. They seized upon the pre-Reformation Church of St. John the Baptist as the most suitable building around which to build their citadel. This was in 1652. Work commenced at once and the town was therefore faced with the task of erecting a completely new church, thus the new Auld Kirk came into being on the site of the then ruined Monastery of the Grey Friars, which had been built in 1472. The Kirk Port was at that time known as Friar's Vennel. On either side of the entrance porch hangs a "mort-safe". This was a contrivance which was placed over a newly buried coffin to prevent the "body snatchers" from taking yet another body; this practice, almost a profession at one time, came to an end on the passing of the Anatomy Act of 1820. Many of Robert Burns's contemporaries are buried here, and a plan of the graveyard hangs in the entrance showing the graves of his friends. Inside the north doorway there are two pillars which it is believed came from the original St. John's. There is a great deal of real interest and beauty inside and outside this fine Auld Kirk.

Loudoun Hall

In Citadel Place is all that remains of the twelfth- or thirteenth-century cruciform church which formed the nucleus of the citadel; it

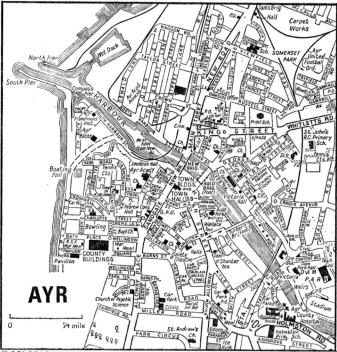

© GEOGRAPHIA LTD.,

is known as the Old Fort, or the Citadel, and consists of the tower only. The church was first mentioned in the thirteenth century but no doubt was considerably older than that; the tower which remains today may have been a later addition. Some small relics of the fort or citadel with heavy gorbell and turret remain on the dockside facing the river. There had been a castle of Ayr, built in 1197, and it is supposed that Cromwell's men used the remaining stone to build their new citadel; in any case there is nothing at all left. Near the river in Fort Street is Loudoun Hall, a fine example of the type of semi-fortified house built by the wealthy during the couple of centuries prior to the union of Scotland and England in 1707. It is open to the public and is one of the most interesting features in Ayr.

The Brigs of Ayr

The New Bridge in Ayr has a special significance in the appellation "new", it was erected in 1878 on the site of the famous "New Brig", renowned in Burns's poem "The Brigs of Ayr"; the old "New Brig" was built in 1789, but lasted only a century. The "Auld Brig", which in 1789 was said to be in a dangerous condition and was considered as ready for demolition, is still there in the latter half of the twentieth century although used for pedestrians only. And so the boast contained in the old verse came true:

> And tho' wi crazy eild I'm sair forfairn,
> I'll be a brig when you're a shapeless cairn.

The Auld Brig is worth a few minutes' study and contemplation of the work of men in the days when quality of workmanship was the all-important factor. Just when it was built is not known for certain, probably in the fourteenth century.

Tam o' Shanter Inn

The Tam o' Shanter Inn on the north side of High Street has strong Burns connections, it was one of his favourite retreats and apparently the inspiration of several of his poems. A call here is well worth while. There are a great many other places in the Burgh of Ayr that should be visited, the Carnegie Library, the Newton Steeple, the old dockside, where a few ships still call, and many other interesting places.

The Burns Monument

Two miles south of Ayr is one of the most famous villages in Southern Scotland: Alloway, the birthplace of Robert Burns. Burns's first home is now the property of the Trustees of the Burns Monument and is open to the public, as is a small museum next door. The

monument itself is a fitting memento to Scotland's famous bard, for it
is contained in a very beautiful garden and surrounded by gnome-like
effigies of many of the characters about whom he wrote. Tam
o' Shanter and Souter Johnnie are probably the most attractive. Kirk
Alloway is no doubt the church where Robert Burns was baptised and
received his first religious instruction. Not a great deal is known of this
old Kirk but it has, of course, been immortalised in "Tam o' Shanter".
On one wall of the Kirk is the following inscription:

> The winnock-bunker in the east
> Where sat auld Nick in shape o' beast.

That sounds very much like the work of Burns himself, but it is not
known who wrote it. However, it is above the eastern gable that the
old bell hangs; it is dated 1657 and bears the inscription "For the Kirk
of Alouay". The Kirk itself is a great deal older than the bell. Although
the date of building is not known it is certainly very early sixteenth or
more probably fifteenth century.

Brig o' Doon
The Brig o' Doon is not only an aged and very beautiful bridge but
was made doubly famous by Burns, for this is the brig over which
Tam had to pass to be freed from the witches. It crosses the Doon at a
point very close to the Burns Monument at a particularly beautiful
stretch of the river. Its age is not known but was probably the
fourteenth century. It is hump-backed, floored with cobbles, and is a
most fascinating and aged piece of stonework.

Greenan Castle
About two miles south of Ayr and right on the coast are the ruins
of Greenan Castle. This is best approached along the sea-shore; if,
however, the visitor goes through Greenan Farm enquiries should be
made as to the best route. Greenan is quite a romantic and fascinating
ruin on a rocky headland exposed to all the north and west winds that
blow across the wide expanse of the lower Firth. Its age is not known
but is almost certainly not younger than 700 years.

"Poosie Nansie"
Two miles from Ayr on the Mauchline road is one of the colleges
of the West of Scotland Agricultural College, where students from all
over the world are taught the rudiments of agriculture. Part of the
buildings were the eighteenth-century Auchincruive mansion house
from which the college takes its name. At Mauchline itself may be seen
the almost unchanged "howff" of Robert Burns—"Poosie Nansie".
This is a fine little place with distant views of Ayr Bay and the coast.

PRESTWICK

Population: 13,500.
Early Closing Day: Wednesday.
Tourist Information Office: Boydfield Gardens, Station Road end.

NOT SO LONG AGO Prestwick and Ayr were two distinct and separate places; today, although still separate Burghs, they are in fact joined by a continual built-up area. Prestwick town centre is about two miles north of Ayr town centre. Both enjoy the same natural advantages, the glorious sands, the gentle climate and good swimming conditions.

International Airport

In the latter half of the twentieth century Prestwick has become known to thousands the world over as a great International Airport. Into Prestwick come the great airliners from all corners of the world, but particularly from across the Atlantic. Prestwick's reputation as a fog-free airport is second to none and has been one of the greatest factors in the progress and rise to fame of this airport, which is second only to Heathrow in the United Kingdom. All the free world is served by the many companies using Prestwick and on one or two occasions this has, for a short while, been the only fog-free airport in the British Isles.

Baronial Burgh

Air traffic is not the only reason for the fame of this once tiny place. As long ago as 900 Prestwick was granted a charter conferring the status of a Baronial Burgh, certainly the oldest Burgh in Ayrshire and the oldest recorded Baronial Burgh in Scotland. No river of any size enters the sea at Prestwick so we can assume that the merchants imported and exported their goods through the port of Ayr, which was a very busy port before the railways caused the death of the smaller harbours and the prosperity of the bigger ones. Little seems to be known of the industry of Prestwick; it was the centre of a thriving agricultural district and in all probability agriculture was the main occupation of the people.

Bruce's Well

A number of saints were associated with Prestwick, St. Ninian, St. Medana and St. Cuthbert, to whom the Parish Church is dedicated. The Mercat Cross is one of the best preserved in the south of Scotland but its age is unknown. It was, however, certainly inexistence long before the sixteenth century. St. Nicholas' Church is without doubt

Tranquil west coast scene

Culzean Castle: one of Scotland's show places

Newton Stewart on the beautiful River Cree

Boat building at Girvan

the oldest in the town and dates from the thirteenth century. It is now roofless but is nonetheless a very interesting and moving remnant. Bruce's Well at Kingcase concerns an age-old legend about Robert Bruce the King of the Scots. On a particular day when he was hard pressed by his enemies he sank wearily to the ground at Kingcase. He was ill, thirsty and desperately weary. He stuck his spear into the ground while he rested and a little later was amazed to see water flowing from the small hole his spear had made. He naturally quenched his thirst and his weariness and sickness left him. In thankfulness he had a well built on the spot as well as a small hospital for lepers. In 1912 the authorities had the well rebuilt but it is interesting to note that right up to that time the original coarse stonework had been kept in good order and the well used. There are many other interesting places to be seen by the visitor with an enquiring turn of mind.

Family Resort

It is as a sister holiday centre to Ayr that Prestwick really comes into its own. Nature has endowed Prestwick with a sandy beach of such dimensions that it can hardly get crowded. The sea here is said to be particularly safe for bathing and so it becomes a paradise for families. The local authorities have enhanced these natural advantages without turning their pleasant town into a noisy twentieth-century Blackpool, a cheerful and fun-loving spot without the noise that so often goes with the modern seaside resort. The Bathing Lake on the sands and Boydfield Gardens are two of the most attractive features from holidaymakers' viewpoint. In Boydfield Gardens displays of all kinds take place while the ever-popular band plays music. One of the greatest attractions of these gardens are the trees. Here at Prestwick the British Open Golf Championship is played out each year. Sailing is a particularly popular sport, while both fresh water and sea angling are increasing in popularity. The visitor's or sightseer's gallery at the airport is another particularly popular spot.

TROON

Population: 11,600.
Early Closing Day: Wednesday.
Tourist Information Office: 14, Templehill.

THIS QUITE MODERN LITTLE TOWN will have particular attractions for the family and for the golfer. Few towns have better sands and bathing facilities, and few towns can offer the golfer more diverse

F

conditions under which to enjoy his particular sport. There are five courses including the Old Troon Championship Course. Apart from sea swimming, which is reputed to be very safe, there is an open pool which is heated. The town itself was, until the late nineteenth century, a small fishing village clustered around the harbour. A little prior to the end of the last century the third Duke of Portland inaugurated large-scale developments and the town is now growing fast. Shipbuilding and repair work are carried out in the harbour and other industrial development is taking place. To a large extent Troon is a planned town and impresses the visitor as such. The estate at Fullarton has been taken over by the council and made into a very beautiful public park. Troon Harbour is a natural haven from the wild weather that can at times beset this coast. Supposed to have had considerable smuggling connections in days gone by, today it is a busy, peaceful and interesting spot. Another attractive place is the Italian Garden laid out with rock pools. Four miles east of Troon is the ancient Castle of Dundonald close to the village of the same name.

Irvine

A little north of Troon there occurs one of the few outcrops of rock along this coast and, from that point on, the sands sweep in a gentle curve for about four miles to the mouth of the River Garnock, close to the Royal Burgh of Irvine, fast developing into a large industrial town. Iron and brass-founding, chemicals, engineering and many other industries are contributing to the growth and prosperity of the centre of the fifth new town in Scotland, which is expected to have a population of 80,000 in 1990.

Irvine

The River Irvine splits the town in two and joins the River Garnock between the town and the sea. Prior to the deepening of the River Clyde in the eighteenth century Irvine was the chief port for Glasgow and the third port in Scotland. Its importance as a port has sadly declined but its overall industrial growth has been little short of spectacular.

Seagate Castle

The Burns Club is one of the oldest in the world. Apart from industry Irvine can offer the visitor excellent sea-bathing, angling and other sports, as well as varied cultural activities. Seagate Castle, once the home of the Eglinton family, is now an interesting ruin. Both the castle and the grounds and gardens have been preserved by the council. Irvine Old Parish Church was rebuilt in 1772–3 and is very well worth a visit.

Golden Sands

Along the sea-front another five miles of golden sands terminates at Saltcoats. Two miles inland is the industrial Burgh of Stevenston with a present population of over 10,000. The Burgh's prosperity is almost entirely due to the Ardeer explosives factory set up in 1873. The industrial growth of the Burgh is expected to continue. History first mentions Stevenston in 1240. During the eighteenth and nineteenth centuries coal-mining was the economic master but this has entirely ceased and been replaced by a more varied industrial activity. Stevenston was granted Burgh status as late as 1952.

SALTCOATS

Population: 15,000.
Early Closing Day: Wednesday.
Tourist Information Office: Town Clerk's Office, Montgomerie Crescent.

AFTER FOUR HUNDRED YEARS of a very varied history Saltcoats has become a first-class holiday resort on the Firth of Clyde, with magnificent views. In the seventeenth and eighteenth centuries ships from Saltcoats traded with the world at large, but, as with so many of the smaller ports, the passing of the sailing ships brought the, at least partial, death of the port. On the east side of the town are the same golden sands that cover so much of Ayrshire's coast. On the west side is Melbourne Park and amusements for children. In between these two is the old harbour from which boats still take visitors for fishing

and pleasure trips. Possibly the principal attraction is the Saltpans
Bathing Station, which is reputed to be one of the best equipped in
Scotland. Saltcoats is particularly well supplied with parks; some are
shared with the neighbouring towns of Stevenston and Ardrossan.
The name Saltcoats no doubt comes from the ancient trade in salt
for which this town was once noted. Immediately west of the town
the Stanley Burn separates Saltcoats from its neighbour Ardrossan.
The very interesting North Ayrshire Museum is situated in the town.

ARDROSSAN

Population: 10,900.
Early Closing Day: Wednesday.
Tourist Information Office: Town Clerk's Office, Burgh Chambers.

NOT MUCH MORE THAN a hundred years ago there was no such
place as Ardrossan. At that time there were the ruins of the ancient
castle and the natural facilities for a harbour—no more. In 1805 the
Earl of Eglinton devised plans for a deep-water harbour and a town
around the ruined castle on its hill-top. In due course these things
came to pass and Ardrossan today is a busy holiday resort and
industrial town with a fine deep-water harbour and a park of no mean
dimensions around the ruins of Ardrossan Castle.

Two Beaches
The town is situated on a small promontory facing the Isle of Arran
with some of the finest views across the Firth. Due to its late arrival,
rather than its gradual growth, Ardrossan is another planned town
with wide orderly streets and a pleasant atmosphere. Of its two beaches,
one on either side of the promontory, the smaller southern one is said
to be the safest for children and bathing, although no dangers are said
to attach to either. The harbour is actually situated at the point of the
promontory. It is a modern and very busy port with an oil refinery,
shipbuilding, a dry dock, and all the equipment for dealing with
general cargo. Ardrossan Harbour is, perhaps, best known to the general
public as the port of embarkation for the Isle of Man, Belfast or the
nearby Isle of Arran, as well as a host of local steamer trips.

Ardrossan Castle
It seems that Ardrossan Castle was built in the twelfth century, but
only some part of the north tower with the central tower and two
dungeons remain. However, the hill, from which are some fine views,

and the grounds around have been converted into a park which adds considerably to the attractiveness of the whole. To the north are the remains of Montfode Castle, about which little or nothing seems to be known. Not far from Ardrossan Castle are the very fragmentary remains of a pre-Reformation church from which has been recovered one of the finest examples of a carved stone coffin in Scotland; it can be seen in the North Ayrshire Museum in Saltcoats.

Sailing Centre

Northwards from Ardrossan the A78 keeps very close to the sea, affording some grand scenery and fine views of Arran as well as the islands and hills farther north. After the tiny village of Seamill is passed the visitor may turn left to Farland Head and the ancient Portencross Castle. Once past the broad Farland Head the road again joins the seafront and the golden sands that stretch away for five miles to Largs. On the way the very small but very pleasant resort of Fairlie is passed. Fairlie is noted for yacht building and has become a favourite sailing centre. From the small pier steamers leave for the Isle of Arran and other Clyde ports.

LARGS

Population: 9,100.
Early Closing Day: Wednesday.
Tourist Information Office: Cumbraen Pavilion.

LARGS IS MAINLY A HOLIDAY RESORT, and indeed is one of the best known on the Ayrshire coast. There are nearly two miles of promenade along the gentle sweeps of the two bays which make up the Largs coastline. Right opposite and only two miles away is the island of Great Cumbrae. The best of the sands is to the south of the town but the whole length of the promenade has interest and fun to offer. Boating and sailing are among the most popular pastimes with swimming and fishing. Boats can be hired and parties are taken for fishing cruises. Steamers leave the pier daily, and for some places more often, for all parts of the Firth of Clyde with connections to other islands. There are special facilities for children, with paddling pool, model yacht pool, sandpits and everything to amuse the younger children. For the grown-up there is just about everything that the visitor can ask for.

Delightful Glen

Among the many places of interest or beauty the visitor will want to visit are the following: the Spring Gardens at Douglas Park and

the flowers at Barrfields Gardens. North of the town is a delightful
glen with a stone and two trees marking the grave of William Smith
and about which there is a story. In the seventeenth century the
plague broke out in Largs and the populace fled to the Glen where
their minister William Smith tended them until he too died and was
buried on the spot. It is said that if ever the two trees meet overhead
the plague will return.

National Recreation Centre

The Skelmorlie Aisle, in the old churchyard off Main Street, is in the
charge of the Dept. of Environment and is regarded as one of the finest
examples in Scotland of Italian architecture; it was built in 1636 as a
mausoleum and contains work of a very high order. By the water's
edge to the north of the town is an outstanding stone pillar named the
Pencil. It commemorates the Scots victory over the Norwegians at the
battle of Largs in 1263. It was erected in 1912. This is a very pleasant
walk past many little bays. The Red Road and Knock Castle is another
fine walk of only five miles. Douglas Park covers fifty acres and rises
to 600 feet above sea-level, with the resultant magnificent views of
which the view of the Firth of Clyde must be one of the finest
panoramas of mountain and sea in Scotland. The National Recreation
Centre of Scotland at Largs was opened in 1958 and commands the
same magnificent views as do other high spots along this attractive
coast. Facilities for most sports, both indoor and outdoor, are provided.
It has the most appropriate name of Inverclyde and is administered by
the Scottish Council of Physical Research. Courses in most sports are
provided and specialist coaches courses are also a part of the
curriculum.

Skelmorlie

Northwards from Largs the road hugs the sea coast all the way to
Greenock, Port Glasgow and Langbank, making this one of the nicest
short runs in the district. Skelmorlie, which is passed just before crossing
the county boundary into Renfrewshire, is a residential area for the
wealthier of the commuters from Glasgow, with as fine a position on
the coastline as one could wish.

THE COAST SOUTH OF AYR

FROM AYR SOUTHWARDS the coastline undergoes a dramatic
change. Past Greenan Castle and around the Heads of Ayr the rocks
protrude in endless little headlands and tiny rocky coves. This is walkers'
country, and following the coast south from Ayr to Girvan would be a

magnificent walk. The road leaves the coast by half a mile to a mile and skirts the edge of the hills, which are not very high and not very interesting until Dunure is reached, about six or seven miles south of Ayr. Dunure is a small fishing village on the main road with a very fine harbour and the ruins of Dunure Castle half a mile away. Now the countryside changes a little; in places the coastal views are fine, in others they are hidden, but shortly the woods of Mochrum appear with Mochrum hill itself peeping over the tree-tops.

Culzean Estate

Here the A719 turns sharp right, leaving the Maybole road on the left, and the visitor enters the really glorious woods of the Culzean (pron. Cul-ane') estate and Castle, both of which are the property of the Scottish National Trust. The very fine Adams Mansion with its host of treasures, the grounds and gardens and the whole lovely picture is entirely exceptional and very symbolic of the age of affluence, but nevertheless one of the show-pieces of Scotland. Walk around the north side of the house and down to the sea at a point where one can look up at the mighty building, where it blends with nature's own magnificence and assumes its rightful place in the scheme of things. Culzean should on no account be missed.

Maidenhead Bay

From Culzean southwards the road keeps well away from the coast through gloriously wooded country, while the coast itself is a magnificent array of rocky headlands and coves. At the village of Maidens in Maidenhead Bay the road meets the sea once more, for the Bay is a popular resort where speedboats and water-skis are in vogue. Maidens was once a small shipbuilding port but now relies on fishing and visitors. The long sandy beach is first class.

Turnberry Castle

The next couple of miles is flat and featureless. On the coast side there is a disused airfield with a track to the lighthouse, and close by on the right, or north, the faint remains of Turnberry Castle, where Robert Bruce was born on 21 May, 1274. Turnberry village is a tiny community living close to the hotel and golf-course at the junction of the A77 and A719.

Coastal Route

For five miles from Turnberry to Girvan the road is closer to the coast and passes many sandy stretches, rocky headlands and tiny coves, and here and there are rough tracks that, with careful driving, enable the motorist to take his car right to the sea-shore.

GIRVAN
Population: 8,000.
Early Closing Day: Wednesday.

GIRVAN IS ALMOST PURELY a holiday resort. A considerable amount of fishing takes place from the excellent harbour and an occasional cargo boat will call. Its two greatest attractions are the beach and adjoining shore-line and the wonderful open country to the west and south. The beach at Girvan makes for safe bathing while north and south of the town are rocky stretches that attract the more energetic. Few steamers call here as they do at so many of the ports on the Firth of Clyde, but the surrounding countryside offers all the exploratory trips imaginable. The steamer trip to Ayr and back is a delight. The most prominent piece of landscape seen from the town and surrounding country is undoubtedly Ailsa Craig, but there is much to attract every type of visitor within a few miles of Girvan.

Paddy's Milestone
The town today is largely nineteenth century but it was here as a small community as far back as the fifteenth century. In the eighteen hundreds the Castle of Ballochtoul was built but was long ago demolished. For many years Girvan held a reputation for boat-building; this lapsed but was recently revived and is once again of some importance. The claim of Girvan to face the Atlantic is perfectly viable for only Ailsa Craig stands in the path of the western breezes and seas. Ailsa Craig, ten miles from Girvan, is often called Paddy's Milestone on the journey from Belfast to Glasgow. It was said in the long ago that it was a stone dropped by the Devil on his way to Ireland. The rock is 1,114 feet high and two miles in circumference and is the home of myriads of sea birds including puffins. Ailsa Craig had a history of smuggling and shipwreck but today its granite is the material used for making curling stones.

Kennedy Pass
Immediately on leaving Girvan the road splits, the A77 along the coast and the A714 southwards across the hills. For twelve to fifteen miles, from Girvan to Ballantrae, the A77 hugs the coast tightly. This is a rock-girt coast and this few miles is one of the most picturesque and delightfully scenic. Some three miles brings the motorist to Ardwell Bay, one of those delightful well-hidden little places that are too small to be mentioned in the local guide. This is Kennedy country and several of the castles inland belonged to that notorious clan. A mile south of Ardwell Bay there is a particularly rugged piece of coastline where the road hugs the cliff-face—this is Kennedy Pass

and for a mile or two southwards there is just room for the road
between the steep hills and the sea.

Carlton Castle

Six miles south of Girvan is the tiny fishing village of Lendalfoot
with a few holiday cottages. This is a lovely little spot with a tiny
harbour and a big reputation from the old days for smuggling.
Dominating the tiny village are the ruins of Carlton Castle high above
the road. Little change occurs in the next few miles, hills on the east
and the sea close by on the west, here and there a stretch of sand
but mostly a rugged coast of great beauty with one or two tiny islands,
in reality rocks above the level of the sea, just off shore. Twelve miles
south of Girvan the small but attractive town of Ballantrae is reached.

Smugglers' Base

With a population of only six hundred and a great reputation as a
holiday centre today and a smugglers' base in the past, Ballantrae is a
delightful spot for a day or a week. The River Stinchar reaches the sea
just to the south of the village and is noted for salmon and trout
fishing. The bridge, age unknown, is certainly worth inspection, as is
the ruin of Ardstinchar Castle, just above the bridge. North, south and
east of Ballantrae is walkers' country—wide open hills with few roads
and many beautiful burns. Not as hard walking as the Highlands, but
sufficiently hard for the average walker, and there are many stretches
of country where a map and compass are essential.

Glenapp Castle

The next ten miles or so southwards to Finnarts Bay is perhaps the
finest run on this west coast route. The road leaves the coast and
descends Glen App through one of the most spectacular and heavily
wooded gorges in Ayrshire. Two miles from Ballantrae is Glenapp
Castle, which should be visited for the gardens and grounds if not
for the Castle itself. At the farthest point the road is nearly three miles
from the coast; this journey of a few miles should be taken slowly in
order to appreciate fully the beauties of the Glen. On reaching
Finnarts Bay at the mouth of the Water of App the visitor has also
reached the southern boundary of Ayrshire. Finnarts Bay is actually
at the entrance to the sea loch of Ryan and is one of the most
attractive spots imaginable—there is virtually no village or other sign
of civilisation, the sea, the bay, the high hill along the coast to the
north and the northern parts of Wigtownshire across the Loch Ryan.
For the walker the coastal route from Ballantrae to Finnarts Bay is to
be highly recommended. It is a rough walk with magnificent views and
an almost complete lack of any sign of the twentieth century.

KILMARNOCK

Population: 48,500.
Early Closing Day: Wednesday.
Market Day: Friday.

KILMARNOCK COMPLETELY DOMINATES the northern half of
Ayrshire. It is an old and important industrial centre. It is the centre
of a wide and varied agricultural district with a market on Fridays. As a
shopping centre it serves the whole area between Cumnock, Ayr, Irvine
and Beith. It is on the main railway line to London and the motorway from
Glasgow to Prestwick Airport. In the seventeenth and eighteenth
centuries Kilmarnock was on the main road from Glasgow to Dumfries,
Carlisle and London. From the above few facts the great importance
of Kilmarnock to the northern end of the county can be easily seen.

> Or, nae reflection on your lear,
> Ye may commence a shaver;
> Or to the Netherton repair,
> An' turn a carpet weaver,
> Aff-hand this day.

From *The Ordination*, by Robert Burns. This verse shows quite
clearly how old and how important is the carpet-weaving industry.
There was a time when weaving, largely bonnets, was almost the only
industry of Kilmarnock; this progressed to carpets and today almost
every type of industry is well represented. The town has the Number 0
Burns Club, the oldest of the many throughout Southern Scotland,
and the Burns Monument is a handsome edifice. "Swift to the Laigh
Kirk one and a'." The Laigh Kirk is still there but only the tower
remains from Burns's time the rest was rebuilt a few years after the
great poet's death. An interesting old town that does not claim to be
a holiday centre, but well and truly worth a stop.

Agricultural Lands

North of Kilmarnock to the Renfrewshire border there are a number
of small industrial towns. To the east the agricultural lands rise
gradually to the hills of Lanarkshire. To the north the same may be
said as the boundary with Renfrewshire is nearly all over 1,000 feet,
and along this border, in between the many towns and villages, is
some lovely open country though in small sections. North of the
Dalry—West Kilbride road there is an area much larger in extent that
should attract the walker; one or two heights rise to 1,500 feet.

Working northwards from Kilmarnock the towns mentioned in the
above paragraph are as follows. **Stewarton,** on the Glasgow—London
line, with a population of around 4,000. It is still known as the
"Bonnet Toon" and has been famous for the making of these bonnets

since the sixteenth century. Today it is almost entirely an industrial town. **Kilwinning** is on the banks of the River Garnock, between Irvine and Stevenston. The once great Abbey is in ruins. The orginal Eglinton Castle was replaced in 1800 by the modern mansion, and the town goes forward into the industrial age but still retains some of its ancient charm in odd places. **Dalry** (population 6,500) is also on the Garnock River and, although old, dates most of its present town from the eighteenth century. The town centre has, fortunately, changed little. This was once a coal-mining and iron town but today has a large number of very diverse industries. Close to the town is Blair Castle, some of which dates from the sixteenth century.

Beith (population 6,000) has a fine reputation for furniture-making but is rapidly changing to plastics, engineering, etc. On nearby Kilbirnie Loch there are facilities for water ski-ing. **Kilbirnie** (population 9,000), on the Irvine to Johnstone road, has a large steel-rolling mill and other factories. Three miles south of Kilmarnock is the tiny village of Craigie with a monument tower commemorating a raid on the town of Ayr in 1297.

Loudoun Castle

About six miles east of Kilmarnock is the pleasant little industrial town of Galston, with a population of over 4,000. It is situated in the Irvine Valley and presents a pleasant picture when approached from Kilmarnock. At the end of the eighteenth century there were eleven mills here. Some thirty to forty years ago half the working population was engaged in coal-mining but this has now ceased. Lace, blanket-making and engineering are the main industries today. On the other side of the River Irvine are the ruins of Loudoun Castle.

Darvel

Farther up the River Irvine and close to the border with Lanarkshire is the comparatively recent town of Darvel, just about 200 years of age. The town's first industries were hand-looms until in the middle of last century a power loom was introduced for lace and madras, which are still the town's main industries.

Distinguished Visitors

About fifteen miles south of Kilmarnock on the A76 is the fast-growing industrial town of Cumnock. Its population is 5,522. Like so many other Ayrshire towns, Cumnock has close associations with Robert Burns as well as with Dr. Johnson and James Boswell. The Mercat Cross, the old Parish Church and the general appearance of Cumnock centre are extremely pleasant; it is a good centre from which to visit all parts of Ayrshire.

Open Country

It is to the south of a line drawn from Ayr to Cumnock that the holiday-maker's Ayrshire really begins; the industrial and semi-industrial have been left behind and ahead, southwards, is fine open country of hills, lochs and burns where the motorist can relax and where the walker can away over the hills to the peace and quietness of nature.

MAYBOLE

Population: 4,600.
Early Closing Day: Wednesday.

MAYBOLE IS THE ANCIENT CAPITAL of the Burgh of Regality of Carrick. It is in an enviable situation, only four miles from the sea and with a truly magnificent view of the hills to the south. There are pleasant parks and recreation grounds, a golf-course, bowling-greens and tennis-courts. In addition Maybole is situated in one of the greenest and loveliest parts of Ayrshire. Three miles south of Maybole on the Dailly road is a village of original character, Crosshill.

Remains of Castles

About eight miles south of Maybole is the one-time pit village of Dailly. It is situated on the Water of Girvan and can be approached by two roads from Maybole; both of these roads follow the very beautiful valley of the Girvan. Near Dailly are the remains of five castles, Killochan, Bargany, Dalquharran, Penkill and Kilkerran. With a good map and a little exploration they can all be found.

Souter Johnnie

Kirkoswald, on the Maybole—Turnberry road, was the home of Souter Johnnie, one of Burns's most famous characters. His cottage is owned by the National Trust for Scotland and contains many interesting relics and furniture of the period. The A77 from Ayr through Maybole and Kirkoswald to the coast is a delight, with green and pleasant country. Or take the A713 from Ayr and follow it through Patna and then along the valley of the River Doon to Dalmelington, with remarkable views of the Galloway Hills, the Carsphairn Kells and Merrick Ranges. A mile south of Dalmelington turn right for Loch Doon; it is about eight miles from the turn-off to the head of the Loch and Doon Castle. Originally the Castle was on a small island in the Loch and the foundations can still be seen, but when the Loch was converted into a reservoir the Castle was removed and rebuilt on the west side of the Loch. This is a very picturesque run.

Forest of Trool

Another absolutely first-class run is to follow the Stinchar River through Colmonell, which is a pretty village with the ruins of Craignell Castle in view on the opposite side of the valley; a footpath can be followed through pleasant scenery to the Castle. Continue to follow the Stinchar River through the dramatic approaches to the high valley village of Barr and on to its source at the head of the Carrick Hills where, at North and South Balloch, the motorist can turn north for Maybole or south through the Nick of the Ballock for the Carrick Hills and the Forest of Trool.

Carrick Hills

One of the finest runs in Ayrshire is from the very old and delightful village of Straiton on the Maybole—Dalmelington road. First see Straiton's fine old church, southwards over some of highest of the Carrick Hills and on through Glen Trool to the main Girvan—Newton Stewart road. Stand on any of the high points on the west side of the Carrick Hills, or west or north of the Forest of Trool, and view the immense sweep of country to the east that shows little if any sign of civilisation—approximately 100 square miles of hill and valley dotted with scores of lochs; and into this very large piece of country, one of the finest tracts of unspoiled land, where virtually only the walker can go. There are a few rough tracks which enter for short distances, but only the walker with map and compass can be at home.

Walking Country

In the extreme south-west corner of Ayrshire there are one or two good runs through pretty villages and a countryside of hills and valleys that are hard to better. The A714 from Girvan through Pinwherry and Barrhill passes through some first-rate scenery. After Barrhill the road splits. Both go to Newton Stewart, but the right-hand road is by far the most scenic. Here again in this corner of Ayrshire there are many scenes and much wonderful country for the walker only.

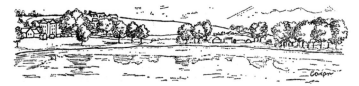

Carlingwark Loch

STRANRAER

Population: 10,000.
Early Closing Day: Wednesday.
Market Day: Friday.

ALTHOUGH GALLOWAY WAS AT ONE TIME a Kingdom with precise and exact boundaries today it is a roughly defined district extending from the River Nith, which enters the sea after passing through Dumfries, to the west coast a few miles beyond Stranraer. From north to south it may be said to include all the country between the Ayrshire border and the sea, with the most southerly point of Galloway and of Scotland at the Mull of Galloway.

Birth of Christianity

A great deal of history attaches to the ancient Kingdom of Galloway, but it is sufficient here to note that the last King of Galloway lived and ruled in the fifteenth century when the people of Galloway were formidable foes of Robert the Bruce, only to become his most ardent adherents in the fight for Scotland's freedom. The Romans were here and left slight remains at Drunmore and Rispain. Whithorn saw the birth of Christianity in these islands. The Vikings, the Saxons and the English all played their part and all have left their own particular contribution to the history of Galloway. But as the far south-west corner of Scotland, somewhat cut off from the industrial centre, her history has a different flavour and so has the countryside in the twentieth century.

Holiday Centre

Stranraer will be best known to thousands as the port for Belfast, but today Stranraer is a fine holiday centre with a history which is really the history of three small villages now combined into the Burgh of Barony of Stranraer. Those three villages were Hillhead, Clayhole and Rawr on the Strand or the Chapel of St. John. It is certain that each of these three have a history connected with the sea, for standing at the head of Loch Ryan, a fine deep-water Loch, would have been appreciated in the earliest days of seafaring.

Safe Bathing

Although Stranraer is less than a hundred feet above sea-level the nearby coast is rock-bound, while inland, north, south, east and west is some of the most varied scenery in Scotland. The town has a lot to offer the visitor: excellent safe bathing, fishing, sailing and most of the attributes of the modern seaside resort. Parks and gardens abound, while the day or half-day trips to Larne in Northern Ireland are becoming more popular each year. There are few old buildings or relics of the history of Stranraer to see, as this is essentially a forward-looking town, but the very slight remains of the Old Castle of St. John may interest some.

Loch Ryan

The road along the east side of Loch Ryan as far as the Ayrshire county boundary, or a little farther to Finnarts Bay, is a fine, and in some places spectacular, run. The little village of Cairnryan, about half-way along the Loch side, will certainly raise questions: it was a naval and military base during the Second World War and has been long disused; it may shortly be developed for industrial purposes. In places along the Loch-side the hills rise nearly sheer and the view across the Loch can be very interesting when ships are leaving or entering.

Corsewall Point

The run up the peninsular on the west side of Loch Ryan is a most interesting trip. Leswalt, the first village is at the base of the Tor of Craigoch, on the summit of which is a tower to the memory of the seventh Baronet of Lochnaw; some views are to be had from this point. Kirkcolm was a seaplane base during the Second World War, and the village is a pretty and quiet spot. The sea of Loch Ryan can be reached by the adventurous motorist at several unfrequented places north of Kirkcolm, and if he is prepared to walk a little, at a number of outstandingly picturesque points on this rock-girt northern coast of the peninsular. The most glorious point of all is Corsewall Point, where the motorist can drive right to the lighthouse and a tiny jetty that must once have had a purpose. On the way the ruins of Corsewall Castle are passed.

Castle of Lochnaw

The west coast offers the same opportunities as the Loch Ryan coast only with a much more rugged coastline. About five miles from Stranraer, by turning left at Leswalt, the two lochs and Castle of Lochnaw will be reached through a very beautiful glen and grounds that are out of the ordinary. The Castle is a Commonwealth Club where guests are welcome. The road to Portpatrick passes through two miles of rhododendrons.

Castle Point

A little farther down the coast and about eight miles from Stranraer is the exceptionally pleasant port and resort of Portpatrick. At one time the port for Northern Ireland and the Royal Mail route, successive storms wrecked the harbour and this trade was lost. There is still a lifeboat station and some fishing. The coastline is one of the boldest in Southern Scotland and the uplands behind the town offer untold opportunities for walking. On Castle Point headland, a mile south of Portpatrick, are the ruins of Dunskey Castle; this is a short and very rewarding walk. The track of the railway that once ran from Portpatrick to Stranraer can be seen beside the Castle. The country east of Portpatrick is largely upland and ranges between open moorland and farming, pleasant without being outstanding.

Port Logan

To continue down the west coast the visitor should visit some of the lesser-known spots which are often reached by tracks that may be rough but usable. Port of Spittal and Port Logan should both be seen. At the latter the famous and exotic gardens should be visited, also the Port Logan Fishpond, which is actually a cavity in the rocks from which and into which the tide ebbs and flows. The cod in this natural aquarium are so tame that they eat from the attendant and sometimes from the hands of visitors. A sandy bay completes the picture of a small but very delightful Port Logan.

Sheltered Beach

Now if the motorist keeps on southwards he will travel along the very narrow peninsular to the most southerly point of Scotland, the Mull of Galloway. On the journey, about seven miles from Portpatrick, the inland scene is one of rocky and picturesque moorland, but the coast-line on the west side is supreme—scores of tiny rock-girt coves and thrusting headlands. Many of these can only be visited by the walker, but the adventurous motorist can see a great deal that the normal visitor misses. Opposite the village of Kirkmaiden the uplands of the west coast tend to get more open, with less agricultural fields, as the peninsula narrows to the few hundred yards at East and West Tarbet and then rises to the headland itself, on the most southerly point of which is the lighthouse. The prospect from this magnificent vantage point is truly breathtaking and should be missed by no one visiting Southern Scotland. At East and West Tarbet, as well as on the headland, there is room for cars and caravans, in fact the

Abbotsford: home of Sir Walter Scott

The Eildon Hills: view from the house

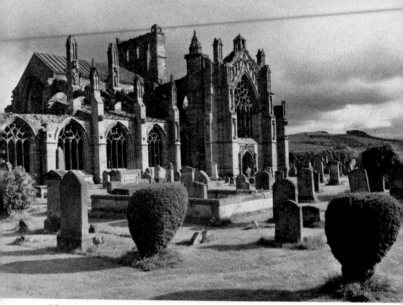

Melrose Abbey: beautiful and romantic ruin

The splendid grandeur of Jedburgh

little beach at East Tarbet can be reached by a narorw track that, with care, will take a caravan. This beach is well sheltered from the west wind.

To the motorist by the main road up the east coast or the coast of Luce Bay Drummore is the next village. Maryport, along a narrow track to the coast, is a caravan and car site only. From Drummore northwards the coast changes to an open beach for miles, not much sand but fine open views across Luce Bay. On this side of the peninsular the land is much more agricultural in character but still very pleasant.

Carved Stones

Opposite Ardwell Chapel Rossan, about a mile inland, are the remains of Killaser Castle, and some two and a half miles farther north is Kirkmadrine, a spot which should not be missed. It is well signposted on the main road between Ardwell Mill and Sandhead Bay, from which place it is two miles. This is the site of one of the earliest Christian churches and the present building is extremely ancient. The most important finds here—carved stones—are housed in an open porch. To the student of early Christianity these stones will be of absorbing interest.

Nature Reserve

The main road continues northwards through the village of Sandhead, which is fast becoming a holiday resort and larger than a village. It is well named, for the sands are fine and continue in an almost unbroken stretch along the north of the Bay to Glenluce. Between the road and the sea there is first an Army rifle range and then a forest and a Nature Reserve, where water fowl are in particular abundance. I have heard it said that some of the sands hereabouts are dangerous, so be careful.

Abbey of Luce

Glenluce, officially known as the largest village in the county, is one of those rather nice friendly places favoured by families. Superb sands, lovely wooded scenery inland, the beautiful Water of Luce, public parks, golf-courses and an extremely friendly atmosphere make Glenluce a place to which to return. Close by and right on the banks of the Water of Luce is the Abbey of Luce, founded by Roland, the Lord of Galloway, in 1190 for the Cistercian Order of Monks. Although it was not wrecked, as were so many, by the Reformers, it has suffered at the hands of other vandals. However, a great deal of interest and beauty remains. It is in charge of the Dept. of Environment and is open to the public. A mile from the village and on the west side of the Water of Luce is the Castle of Park; it stands in a romantic and picturesque

G

spot but should be viewed from the outside, for it is very unsafe. To
reach it rurn right immediately after crossing the river and passing
under the railway viaduct.

Penwhirn Reservoir

The country around is agricultural and slopes gently down from the
high hills to the north. There are two roads northwards out of
Glenluce, the most westerly follows the Water of Luce to the pretty
village of New Luce, where, by turning left, it may be followed along
a narrow and delightful road over the hills to its source in Ayrshire,
passing the Penwhirn Reservoir. In this particular stretch of country
the adventurous motorist can really have fun, for there are several
rough tracks which may, or may not, be suitable for a car. From New
Luce the motorist can continue northwards to Ayrshire, but for the
walker this is fine going with long open miles ahead. The road which
leaves Glenluce to the north-east is of the type with much the same
attractions, leading past Loch Ronald to the River Bladnock and the
Penninghame Forest and eventually to the B7027 which, followed
northwards, passes within easy distance of many lochs and into
Ayrshire, or southwards to the Stewartry of Kirkcudbright. All the
country north of Glenluce tends to take on more and more a moorland
character as one travels north, but no great heights are reached until
the Forest of Trool and the Carrick Hills are approached. Two miles
north-east of Glenluce are the ruins of the Castle of Carscreugh, which
was immortalised by Sir Walter Scott in *The Bride of Lammermoor*.

Whithorn Peninsula

Southwards from Glenluce the A747 will carry the visitor into the
most ancient cradle of Christianity in these islands. The road down the
west side of the Whithorn Peninsula follows very close to the sea with
the moors above, pleasant but not spectacular. Some six or seven
miles from Glenluce turn left to Mochrum Loch, Castle Loch and
several other very picturesque lochs which had associations with
Robert the Bruce. A mile and a half beyond the turn-off for Mochrum
is Chapel Finnian; it consists of a small enclosure and the remains of a
tiny chapel built by St. Finnian in the sixth century at one of the
places where pilgrims probably landed. It is a most moving remnant of
early Christian history. The well still survives after thirteen centuries.

St. Ninian's Cave

The next little village of importance is Port William, with a nice little
harbour, golf, tennis, swimming and boating. Nearby is the White Loch
of Myrton Bird Sanctuary. On the south side of the loch are the ruins
of Myrton Castle. Seven miles from Port William, on the main Isle of

Whithorn road, is a notice which says "St. Ninian's Cave". Follow
the narrow road to the farm and then the signpost for a walk of a mile
and a half, a most pleasant walk, to the cave that was used by St.
Ninian in the sixth century; many carved stones were found here and
are now in the Museum at Whithorn. Next to the cave are the ruins of
Port Castle on the opposite side of the small burn. This piece of coast
is walkers' country and should be walked from Port William to the Isle
of Whithorn; at places it is two miles from the road but never very far
from a farm.

Stinking Harbour

The Isle of Whithorn, which, by the way, is no longer an island, is
famous as the site of St. Ninian's Chapel. The present small church is
probably thirteenth century but the remains of a very much earlier
chancel were discovered. It is presumed that the Isle was a landing-
place for pilgrims and that the church or chapel provided a light to guide
vessels into the port as well as, of course, a place of worship. The
Dept. of Env. official guide book makes absorbing reading. In
later years the Isle of Whithorn achieved notoriety as a smugglers'
rendezvous. At that time the roadway was well under water at high
tide, but the new road has formed a dry causeway. There are two little
harbours, the one on the west is the Isle of Whithorn harbour, the one
on the east side is known as the Stinking Harbour, sometimes the
False Harbour. Many years ago there was a lifeboat of the old-fashioned
sailing and rowing type. Fishing among the few fishermen left is
almost entirely for crabs and lobsters with "a few salmon when no one
is looking". The square tower on the headland was a coastguard
lookout. This is a fascinating little place that warrants a few hours'
exploration. Three miles from the Isle and about two and a half miles
from the coast is Whithorn village, of more ancient fame than possibly
any other place in Scotland. It is a matter of controversy as to whether
St. Ninian's Priory of the late fourth or early fifth century actually
existed at the Isle or at Whithorn village. It is generally agreed that the
first church, Candida Casa, the White Church, was on the Isle of
Whithorn and that the eventual Priory was at the village. No proof
exists but both places were among the very first to receive the earliest
Christian missionaries. The remains of the Priory and the Museum,
which houses many crosses and carved stones found in the area, are
more than interesting, and to the student will be an essential visit.

Cruggleton Castle

The coast road up the east side of the peninsula touches the coast
at one or two points only. Cruggleton Castle, on a headland three
miles from Whithorn, and once the stronghold of the Comyns, should

be seen; it entails a very short walk. Inland is fairly flat agricultural land of no particular significance but pleasant enough. There are many spinneys dotted about and many side roads for the enquiring motorist to explore. Garlieston, a few miles north, is lucky to have the most superb bay, a tiny picture-book harbour and a great headland across the bay. A very pleasant little spot for those seeking peace and quiet. Once Garlieston was a busy port but, as with so many others, the little harbours have had to give way to the bigger ones.

WIGTOWN

Population: 1,154.
Early Closing Day: Wednesday.

WIGTOWN, THE OLD COUNTY TOWN of Wigtownshire, received its charter creating it a Royal Burgh in 1341. It is built on a hill, the southern slopes of Penninghame Ridge, and overlooks the sands of Wigtown Bay. At one time it was a port of great importance, but the harbour is now completely silted up and derelict. The River Bladnoch flows into the estuary of the Cree and the Bladnoch a little south of the town. On Windy Hill, which overlooks the Bay, is a monument to two women Covenanters who were tied to stakes on the sands and drowned by the incoming tide. The town is one of the tidiest and nicest with a Mercat Cross and another very ancient cross. The County Buildings, at one side of the square, which contains a handsome garden, are outstanding in red and white freestone with a tall clock tower. The old Parish Church is in ruins but is still very well

Newton Stewart, Cree Brige

worth inspection. Baldoon Castle, or the ruins thereof, are a mile south of the town next to a farm, and on the side road to the Crook of Baldoon is another ruined tower.

Penninghame Ridge

Wigtown is a very pleasant little town and a good centre for the motorist, but the immediate surrounding countryside is pleasant but not spectacular in any way. The run to Newton Stewart, some seven miles, passes over Penninghame Ridge from which there are some fine views. Inland along the Bladnoch River is good farming country and even the Penninghame Ridge never rises over 500 feet. It is, however, a green and well-watered landscape.

NEWTON STEWART

Population: 2,000.
Early Closing Day: Wednesday.
Market Day: Wednesday.
Tourist Information Office: Machars Tourist Board,
Dashwood Square.

THE ANCIENT CLACHAN OF NEWTON is situated on the west bank of the River Cree, a particularly beautiful river, and assumed the name Newton Stewart and the dignity of a Burgh of Barony in 1677, when William Stewart of Castle Stewart was granted a charter by Charles II. The River Cree forms the boundary between the Shire of Wigtown and the Stewartry of Kirkudbright and, in its upper reaches, from the ancient Lordship of Carrick. In the town there is much to see: the Town House, of particularly Scottish design and white in colour, is one of the finest buildings of its kind. The handsome bridge across the Cree was built in 1813 from local granite.

Glen Trool

There are three roads northwards from Newton Stewart. The A714 follows the west bank of the River Cree and remains very close to that river through delightful scenery to Bargrennan Cairn, where the motorist can continue along the main road, skirting the Carrick Hills, to Ayrshire and Girvan, or, he can turn right along a side road to Glentrool village, Glen Trool and Loch Trool, set in the most spectacularly beautiful scenery in Southern Scotland. There is no other area to compare with Glen Trool and the Forest of Trool. If at the village of Trool the motorist keeps to the right he will come to the eastern end of the Loch, ample parking space, and have arrived at the starting point for some of the finest walks in completely wild and open country, where a map and compass are absolutely necessary. If at Glentrool village the motorist keeps to the left he will cut right through the Forest of Trool and the Carrick Hills, at the beginning of which he can turn right for Straiton or left for Maybole, both in Ayrshire. Either of these routes is a trip not to be forgotten easily and not to be repeated elsewhere in Southern Scotland.

Walkers' Paradise

There is a narrow road which follows the east bank of the Cree to Glentrool; some may prefer this quieter road. The B7027 leaves the A714 two miles west of Newton Stewart and, passing through Penninghame Forest and close to Loch Ochiltree and the Loch of Fyntalloch, continues over the Ayrshire boundary to Barrahill and Girvan; this is a lovely run, but not to be compared with the Forest of Trool or the Carrick Hills, where the watershed is reached at nearly 1,500 feet amid some of the grandest and wildest scenery, hill upon hill as far as the eye can see, and all this country is studded with lochs. A walkers' paradise it is indeed.

Grey Mares Tail

Cross the River Cree at Newton Stewart and take the A712 for New Galloway. Through the southern reaches of Kirroughtree Forest, between hills rising to nearly 2,000 feet, past the "Grey Mares Tail", a magnificent 80-foot waterfall, past Clatteringshaws Loch and downhill to New Galloway on the Water of Ken. This is another supremely beautiful run with scenery that, in places, is hard to beat, and all the way there is plenty of room for picnicking and caravans.

Rusko Castle

Southwards along the east bank of the Cree brings the visitor to Creetown, the Ferritown of *Guy Mannering*, and famous long ago for its granite quarries. This road, which closely follows the coast, is a very pleasant and sometimes picturesque run; it passes the ruins of Carsluith Castle and Dirk Hatteraick's Cave (read Scott's *Guy Mannering*) and runs through much lovely wooded country to Gatehouse of Fleet on the Water of Fleet. There is another and much more attractive road to Gatehouse of Fleet: turn left at Creetown and follow the road which runs alongside the Moneypool Burn and close to the old railway-track. After the old railway station for Gatehouse of Fleet watch for the ruins of Rusko Castle on the left, about three and a half miles from the station. From the castle the road follows the Water of Fleet into the town. In this circle of land, perhaps five miles in circumference, are hills that rise well over 1,000 feet and few habitations or signs of civilization, and across the middle runs the old Military Road, in part called the Corse of Slakes. This should be a fine walk and may be passable by motor-car. North of the old railway line the country is virtually uninhabited hill and forest, rising to well over 2,000 feet, with scores of burns and several lochs. This type of country continues across the New Galloway road and northwards.

GATEHOUSE OF FLEET

Population: 950.
Early Closing Day: Thursday

THE TWO NAMES STEWARTRY OF KIRKCUDBRIGHT and Gatehouse of Fleet raise questions of origin. The first is known with certainty. Archibald Douglas, known as "Archibald the Grim", in the fourteenth century received from the King all the lands of Galloway between the Rivers Nith and Cree. Douglas, being a very busy man, appointed a steward to administer these lands and so it became known as the Stewartry, and the name is still used today. Gatehouse of Fleet may have meant the gateway to the estates of the nearby Cally, whose owners have for long been Lairds of the district. Or it may have been a gate or post with a turnpike for the collection of tolls on the road between Carlisle and Portpatrick, which came into being in 1642 largely as a military road for transport of troops. Very soon after its opening the coaches and post-riders also used it. In places the present road follows the old but in places the old road is a green track which makes for wonderful walking. The forerunner of the present bridge over the Water of Fleet was built in 1661 by Richard Murray. The name Gatehouse of Fleet should apply to the district and not just the town which actually consists of two parishes, Anworth on the west and Girthon on the east.

This little town has had a most interesting history, in fact the town did not come into existence until about 1760, when James Murray, a descendant of the bridge-builder, introduced the cotton industry on the banks of the Fleet. The water to drive the wheels which supplied the power was brought from Loch Whinyeon by an aqueduct, the remains of which can be seen today. Soon other industries followed and in 1795 Fleet became a Burgh of Barony. A small harbour was built at Boat Green and a 1,400-yard canal was cut to lessen the length of the twisting river. This enabled ships of 300 tons to use the harbour and shipbuilding soon followed. The present Anworth Hotel was the Ship Inn. With the coming of the railways in the middle of last century the industries died gradually and Gatehouse of Fleet became the quiet and rather charming little town of the twentieth century.

Anworth Old Kirk

The most outstanding building in the town is the square clock tower built of Craignair granite in 1871. Anworth Old Kirk is situated in the beautiful wooded Anworth Glen, and in addition to the very considerable remains of the Old Kirk contains the family crypt of the Maxwells of Cardoness Castle. Girthon Old Kirk is about two miles south of Gatehouse on the road to Sandgreen. Only the walls are now standing but it is either a Norman or Early English period church. Both churches contain the graves of Covenanters and both entail a very pleasant walk.

Cardoness Castle, now in the hands of the Dept. of Environment, is on the coast close to the main Creetown road and about three miles south of Gatehouse. It was built in the middle of the fifteenth century and belonged at various times to the McCullocs, Gordons and Maxwells. Considering its age this castle is in extremely good order, as is Rusko Castle on the B796 and about three miles north of the town. Rusko was for a long time in the hands of the Gordons of Lochinvar and it is said that it was to Rusko that Young Lochinvar brought his bride. In the immediate district there are many delightful walks and short motor runs.

Castle Haven Bay

The main road, the A75 to Castle Douglas, should be left at its junction with the A755 about three miles from Gatehouse for Kirkcudbright; this is a pleasant but not spectacular run. By far the most interesting route is to stick as close to the coast as possible. Visit Sandgreen, the National Trust for Scotland coastline at Carrick, Castle Haven Bay, once the haunt of smugglers, and the ruined dungeons of the castle, which are all that can be seen today. Beautiful and little-frequented places along this broken and rock-girt coastline make this a more than usually interesting coastal exploration. Finally the motorist enters Kirkcudbright along the banks of the River Dee.

KIRKCUDBRIGHT

Population: 2,711.
Early Closing Day: Thursday.

KIRKCUDBRIGHT, THE NAME IS PRONOUNCED kirk-koo'bree, a Royal Burgh, is one of the most ancient and historic towns in Southern Scotland. Tradition has it that the name comes from St. Cuthbert, which was one of the stopping places of the Monks of

Lindisfarne on their epic journey which was to finish at Durham. Nothing of the very ancient Kirk of St. Cuthbert remains but traces of an earlier church than the fifteenth century Greyfriars church, which can be visited and examined today, as can St. Cuthbert's churchyard.

Maclellan's Castle

Kirkcudbright probably has a greater percentage of fine old houses of the seventeenth century than any other town in Galloway. But of course there are older remains by far. Close to the river and surrounded by gardens and tall trees is a flat-topped mound that may have been a natural hillock before the first Castle of Kirkcudbright was built on the summit; this has long ago disappeared completely but was replaced in the sixteenth century by Maclellan's Castle, which is a more than usually interesting castle of the period.

Broughton House

The very old building at the end of High Street with a tower and a really beautiful spire is the Tolbooth, built in 1626. It is admittedly a plain but very distinguished building with the mark of age in every stone. John Paul Jones was in one of the cells here for a period on a charge of murder; however, the charges were not pressed and he was released. At the top of the Tolbooth is the cell which Sir Walter Scott portrayed as the cell in which Glossin met her death by the hands of the pirate and smuggler Dirk Hatteraick. Outside hang the "jougs", a fairly common punishment in the early days. Broughton House is another fine example of early eighteenth-century architecture. And there are many more for the visitor with a discerning eye.

Billy Marshall

A very long while ago Kirkcudbright was one of the most important ports on the Solway, but the old harbour silted up and ships went elsewhere. A breastwork was built along the river front and the old harbour is now Harbour Square. However, a little farther upriver, beyond the unsightly concrete bridge, is a small modern harbour where small tankers unload oil. One of the most curious monuments in the town is the stone erected to the memory of Billy Marshall (1672–1792), a famous gipsy who died at the age of 120 years. Billy had fought in the King's army at the Battle of Boyne 102 years before his death.

Meikle Ross

Only a mile from the town is the tiny village of Kirkchrist with the ruins of the pre-Reformation church. It has connections with *Old Mortality*, and very close by was a distillery which caused Robert Burns to refer to Kirkcudbright as Whisky Jean. Farther south along the coast are the ruins of Balmangan Tower and Senwick Church. For over two miles the coast is lined with woods to Ross Bay and the great headland of Meikle Ross. From here some wonderful views up and down the Solway can be had as well as many delightful views inland. From the hill church of the village of Borgue are some more fine views. A little north of Kirkcudbright is the village of Tongland, with a most interesting and probably ancient bridge across the Dee.

Varied Scenery

The New Galloway road northwards from Kirkcudbright provides good motoring and scenery of a very varied and beautiful kind as far as the village of Lauriston, where the motorist can turn left for Gatehouse along one of the finest and most scenic hill roads in the county. Turn right for Castle Douglas or straight on for Lauriston Forest, Woodhall Loch and the tiny hamlet of Mossdale at the southern end of Loch Ken. From here northwards the road follows the loch-side with Cairn Edward forest almost pushing the road into the loch, along the Water of Ken and through the popular New Galloway and St.

Kirkcudbright, Carrick Shore

Johns, Town of Dalry, still along the Water of Ken to Carsphairn, Dalmellington and Loch Doon. This run takes the motorist through some of the wildest of the southern highlands with unequalled scenes of hill and valley dotted with lochs. Side roads invite the exploring motorist into the wilder spots that are never crowded.

A Pleasant Run

The main road can be followed to Castle Douglas, a distance of about nine miles. This is a good road and quite a pleasant run but the discerning motorist will follow the side road through Dundrennan and see the Abbey, founded in 1142. It is one of the most beautiful remains in this part of Scotland. On this road there are many lanes running down to the sea at delightful spots: Abbey Burnfoot, Rascarrel Bay, Balcary Point, Auchencairn Bay and the pleasant old village of Palnackie, where the old and disused harbour is worth inspection. Half a mile north of Palnackie take the side road on the left for Castle Douglas, through a green and lovely country. There are many other roads that could have been used from Dundrennan to Castle Douglas; all pass through green country with the hills away from the coast.

CASTLE DOUGLAS

Population: 3,265.
Early Closing Day: Thursday.
Market Days: Monday, Tuesday, Thursday.
Tourist Information Office: Markethill.

CASTLE DOUGLAS IS CERTAINLY ONE of the nicest towns in the south-west and its main attraction today will be the Lochside caravan park and camping ground. Few other such sites can compare with the glorious flower-beds, the tree-lined loch and the high hills to the south.

Archibald the Grim

The first inhabitants of this district no doubt lived on the hills around the loch. The Romans were here, and no doubt many others, but the first records are of Buchan, still a pretty hamlet on the western shores of Carlingwark Loch. Archibald the Grim was the first Douglas to be Lord of Galloway and for over a hundred years this family were among the most powerful in Scotland; they ruled with an iron hand from the Castle at Threave. The great cannon, Mons Meg, now on the ramparts at Edinburgh Castle, was reputed to have been forged at Buchan. It was Sir Walter Scott who in the 1800s was responsible

for the move to preserve this historic piece of artillery. During the
seventeenth and eighteenth centuries there were several villages in the
immediate neighbourhood, including Carlingwark, which in 1792
became the Burgh of Barony of Castle Douglas. It was a Douglas, but
not one of the Threave family, that was responsible for the town's
start on the road to prosperity. Today it is a prosperous market town
and centre for the fine agricultural district around.

Carlingwark Loch

Sailing and rowing on Carlingwark Loch are free of charge unless
one hires a boat; heavy, fast-powered boats are forbidden, which is a
great attraction. Coarse fishing is another free sport in the Loch. As a
shopping centre Castle Douglas can please most and as a centre for
the motoring runs as well as for the keen hill-walker it is hard to beat.

Water of Ken

Among the many lovely runs from Castle Douglas is the road which
follows the River Dee and the east bank of Loch Ken to New
Galloway and St. John's Town of Dalry; a right turn can be made for
the return trip at New Galloway, St. John's Town of Dalry or a few
miles farther north before entering Carsphairn. The road along the east
bank of the Water of Ken from Dalry to Carsphairn presents probably
one of the finest panoramas of hill country in the Stewartry. North of
the A712 and west of the A762 is where the walker and the exploring
type of motorist will find the greatest rewards. Take the side roads
and leave the main roads to those who merely wish to get from A to B.

Threave Castle

Before leaving Castle Douglas there are two places that must be
visited. Threave Garden belongs to the National Trust for Scotland
and, apart from being one of the most varied and beautiful, is a
gardening school. It is quite impossible to describe adequately the
gardens in their colourful beauty during the spring and summer.
Woodlands, a walled garden, rose garden, vegetables and a rock
garden are just a few of the different types of horticultural artistry
that can be seen. The whole of the Threave Estates including farms is
a wild-fowl refuge or bird sanctuary and was presented to the National
Trust for Scotland by Major Gordon in 1948. Take the A75 westwards
from Castle Douglas and, after following the loch-side, turn down a
narrow lane which is signposted on the right-hand side of the road
about half a mile from the loch; this will lead to Threave Castle on an
island in the River Dee; a boat will ferry visitors across. This was the
ancestral home of the Douglas family, often called the Black
Douglases. It is an astonishingly complete castle of its type, and it

was built in the 1300's. Its position adds to the pleasure of the quite easy visit.

This powerful Clan of the Douglases had many colourful characters in its annals. Often the Earls of Douglas were close to the sovereigns, but almost as often they were at war with them, despite their famous badge of the loyal 'Douglas Heart'. The more sinister side of the 'Black Douglases' is enshrined in an old ballad which comments on their fierce deeds which were always:

> Making king and people grieve,
> Oh, the lawless lords of Galloway,
> Oh the bloody towers of Threave!

Dalbeattie

Population: 3,231.
Early Closing Day: Thursday.

From whichever direction one enters this attractive little town the picture is of a church spire, houses of granite backed by the forested slopes with the high heather hills overlooking all. It is often called the Granite Burgh. It was not until 1780 that the town as we know it came into being. The granite quarries close by brought great prosperity to the town, which itself is built of granite. There are some lovely parks but the surrounding countryside provides the real reason for the popularity of Dalbeattie.

Orchardon Tower

About five miles south of the town, past the village of Palnackie is Orchardon Tower, of fifteenth century origin, but peculiar in being circular; it is in excellent order and very interesting. Immediately west of the town and right alongside the Urr Water are the remains of the Castle of Buittle in a delightful spot between two woods and two hills. It was probably built sometime in the twelfth century and belonged to the Balliols; it was a much stronger and larger castle than now appears.

Unfrequented Spots

Where the Urr and the Dalbeattie Waters join forces is the old and completely disused port of Dalbeattie; the landing-stage with bollards can be seen. Four miles north on the A710 is the village of Haugh of Urr, from where some delightful short walks can be taken. Kippford is the nearest seaside resort to Dalbeattie and is well patronised. It has a fine position on the estuary of the Urr and faces some glorious scenery on the opposite bank, backed by the 1,200 feet of Bengairn and Screel. At one time Kippford was a small port and did a little shipbuilding. Next door are Castle Point and Rockcliffe Bay, two delightfully unfrequented spots.

Beinloch Hill

Apart from the several side roads there are two ways to Dumfries from Dalbeattie. The A711 passes Corro Castle, Lochanhead and close to Mabie Forest and finally along the old Military Road into Dumfries. The more exciting and scenic is by the coast road. After passing the two side turns to Kippford and Rockcliffe the almost sheer sides of Beinloch Hill are passed, and then with open hill land on the left or north the flats which stretch from a little east of Sandyhills Bay to Dumfries provide a good deal of interest as well as glimpses of some beautiful scenery among the hills on the north and west side.

Paul Jones

At Southerness Point is a lighthouse as well as a hotel and caravan camp. Turn right at the little village of Kirkbean for Abigland, where Paul Jones was born in the middle 1700's, and after a period in the English Merchant Navy, during which he became a captain at the age of twenty-one, he went to America and fathered the navy during the War of Independence. The cottage where he was born is still there. There is much more to be found on this coast with the help of a map and a gift for exploration.

Sweetheart Abbey

After passing under the towering height of Criffell, New Abbey is reached, with the very extensive remains of Sweetheart Abbey. This lovely place was founded by Devorgilla, the wife of John Balliol, in 1273. It was the last Cistercian foundation in Scotland and was colonised from Dundrennan. Of all the Abbeys in Southern Scotland this one is most worth seeing. It has the reputation of being one of the most beautiful of Scottish Abbeys. John Balliol was the founder of Balliol College, Oxford, and when he died his wife Devorgilla remained in Galloway and devoted herself to helping the poor. She is said to have carried her husband's heart in a casket and to have been buried with it in Sweetheart Abbey, which was so named on account of her devotion.

From New Abbey to Dumfries there is nothing of particular interest until one crosses the Nith by the most northerly of the two bridges from Maxwelltown, where Devorgilla founded a monastery for Grey Friars, into Dumfries. This bridge or its ancestor was built by Devorgilla especially for the use of the Grey Friars.

Section 6   Scott's Country and The Border

DUMFRIES

Population: 29,200.
Early Closing Day: Thursday.
Market Day: Wednesday.
Tourist Information Office: Whitesands.

DUMFRIES IS ONE OF THOSE attractive towns that call for exploration. Very little is known of the early history of Dumfries but by 1186 there was a Royal Castle at Castledykes and the first St. Michael's Church was in being. In the late thirteenth century a Monastery was founded by Devorgilla on the west side of Castle Street between Friars Vennel and Buccleugh Street. The present Greyfriars' Church was completed in 1868 and has no connection with the Monastery.

Burns Museum

Although Robert Burns was born near Ayr this is the Burns town; wherever one goes there is a reminder of the great poet. In 1787 he was made a burgess, and shortly afterwards he moved to Ellisland Farm about six miles to the north on the Kilmarnock road. It was here that he wrote *Tam o' Shanter*. The farm is open to visitors. In the house in which Burns died is a museum of absorbing interest, including a record of the poet's descendants to the present day. Quite close to this house is St. Michael's churchyard, with the very beautiful mausoleum containing his remains. At the Globe Inn, one of the most frequented haunts of Burns, there is a great deal of interest. The statue of Burns at the northern end of High Street, with the poet sitting on a tree-stump, is in white marble and surrounded by flower-beds.

Camera Obscura

The most dominating building in the town is the Midsteeple, built in 1707 as a courthouse and prison. The Burgh Museum is housed in the windmill on the summit of Corberry Hill, which was built in 1798.

Apart from the many items of profound interest the Camera Obscura
is a great attraction. In the small gardens attached is a statue of Scott's
Old Mortality. At the eastern end of the medieval bridge, which itself is
worth inspection, is another museum, the Old Bridge House, displaying
furniture and living conditions from the sixteenth century.

June Festival

Each year on a Saturday in June Dumfries celebrates its historic
past with the Festival named Guid Nychburris, and re-enacts the
ceremony of the Royal Charter granted by Robert III.

Fine Remains

Lincluden Abbey or College was founded in about 1164, and the
architectural remains are very fine and delightfully situated. The
Abbey is in the hands of the Dept. of Environment and open to the
public. It is about two miles from the centre of Dumfries on the
Maxwelltown side of the river.

Caerlaverock Castle

Dumfries can be made the starting point for excursions to many
places of interest and beauty. Glencaple, on the mouth of the Nith,
where the very old occupation of "Haff Net" salmon fishing can be
seen, should be visited. At the right time the Solway bore in all its
fury can also be seen. Some three miles farther south is Caerlaverock
Castle, possibly the finest remains of a thirteenth-century Scottish
castle. It had two moats and is in a most outstanding situation. In
Caerlaverock Churchyard are the remains of Robert Patersen, Scott's
Old Mortality. Another four or five miles bring the visitor to Ruthwell
and the site of the finest Saxon Cross in existence. The intricate
carving tells the story of the life of Christ and is a preaching cross,
not a churchyard memorial, as is the famous Bewcastle Cross in
Northumberland. It was carved and set up in about A.D. 680.

Oldest Post Office

Northwards along the River Nith is some of the most beautiful
country in the county of Dumfries. Take the A76 as far as New Bridge
and there turn left along the B729 for Dunscore and Moniaive, with
a Market Cross dated 1635 and a monument to the last covenanters
executed in 1688. This is a lovely village with the cottages built right
up to the road edge. A turn-off can be made at Kirkland to return by
Penpont and Sanquhar, with the oldest Post Office in Great Britain,
dated 1763, and numerous delightful villages along the heavily
wooded valley of the Nith. The bridge at Auldgirth is well worth
noting.

Daer Reservoir

Another good run is along the A709 to Lochmaben, which has a loch popular with yachtsmen, a castle on Castle Loch and the Torthorwald Cottage Museum. Good angling can be had and the setting is superb. Turn northwards up the B7020 for Moffat, passing over Beattock *en route*. Thus far the countryside has been agricultural, green and pleasant, but once past Beattock and the Forest of Ae, a mile or two to the west, the country opens out into wide open hills and burns with the Daer Reservoir in the centre. These are the Lowther Hills, which form the boundary with Lanarkshire. The A702 runs right across these hills, affording wonderful views; it runs from Elvanfoot in Lanarkshire southwards to the River Nith. Many side roads enter the Lowther Hills and enable the motorist to see the best of the scenery, but the walker has all the advantages.

MOFFAT

Population: 2,000.
Early Closing Day: Wednesday.
Tourist Information Office: Town Clerk's Office.

MOFFAT HIGH STREET, THE MOST IMPORTANT street in the town, is wide handsome and very attractive, with some fine buildings. At the north end is the Colvin Fountain, surmounted by a ram, a symbol of the chief farming activity of the area. The Town Hall is a fine piece of Adam architecture. At the old Kirkyard is a monument to the two Post Office men who lost their lives in the great storm of 1831 in an endeavour to get the mails through to Edinburgh.

Megget Stone

The chief glory of Moffat is the countryside. Six miles north of Moffat the Tweed rises to flow north and east. Some miles north-east of the town, in the wildest of hill country, the Moffat Water rises and joins the Elvan Water from Lanarkshire, a little south of Moffat. Take the A701 north from the town and follow the Tweed from its smallest beginnings. At Tweedsmuir turn right along a side road that climbs to nearly 1,500 feet at the Megget Stone, with a stupendous view of the Talla Reservoir and the long Valley leading to the Tweed or the Yarrow and St. Mary's Loch. From this point the hills, in all directions, are seemingly endless. The A74 from Moffat passes through a much shorter area of hill country to Elvanfoot. On both roads there are side tracks that will attract the more adventurous and the walker. The road

H

along St. Mary's Loch and the Yarrow can be followed to Selkirk, Galashiels and Melrose. A little east of St. Mary's Loch the B709 crosses the Selkirk Road and traverses this same hill country southwards to Lockerbie or Langholme, or eastwards to Hawick. By any of these roads the motorist can see the best of the hills with side tracks and footpaths leading into the lesser-known and frequently most beautiful spots.

SELKIRK

Population: 5,700.
Early Closing Day: Thursday, Saturday.
Tourist Information Office: Halliwell's Close, Market Place.

OF ALL BORDER TOWNS Selkirk is the most important. It takes its Common Riding seriously and cherishes its past. Situated on the River Ettrick, rising to 600 feet in places, Selkirk is said to be the "Ancient Haunt of Kings" and it certainly has had a close association with Royalty through the ages. When David I ascended the throne in 1124 he referred to Selkirk as the "old town". The Monks of Kelso Abbey received their charter at Selkirk and later moved to Kelso. The greatest name in Selkirk's history is Sir Walter Scott, who was a magistrate here, the Sheriff or Shirra of Selkirk. The courtroom still contains the bench and chair from which he presided. In front of the Town Hall is the statue to his memory. In the days when the law was hard and punishment severe the Shirra was one of the kindest and least severe of law officers. The Auld Kirk, which stands on the site of a still older church, was the scene of the proclamation of Sir William Wallace as Overlord of Scotland. In the Public Library Museum there is still preserved an English pennon captured at the Battle of Flodden in 1513. A curfew bell is tolled every night at 8 p.m. as it has for many centuries.

GALASHIELS

Population: 12,250.
Early Closing Day: Mainly Wednesday.

GALA, AS GALASHIELS IS KNOWN LOCALLY, is lucky in its position on the Gala Water, a situation of great beauty, yet the townspeople have done much to preserve the gifts of nature; trees and flowers meet the visitor at every turn. Galashiels is the home of

Tweeds, a name resulting from a clerical error and not from the name of the great river. Tweels was the old Scottish name for woollen fabrics. Accidentally spelt Tweed, the new name stuck and is today known all over the world. This is the largest single industry in the town and has been here since 1662. Here is the Scottish College of Textiles. This was, of course, a town that Sir Walter Scott knew well. Much of his finest work was done at Ashiestiel, where he lived before moving to Abbotsford; among these were *The Lay of the Last Minstrel, The Lady of the Lake, Marmion* and the first few chapters of *Waverley.* But as with Selkirk it is the surrounding countryside that is the real attraction of Gala and the Gala Water.

Tushielaw Tower

Five miles up the Ettrick Water from Selkirk is Ettrickbridgend, a favourite spot with fishermen, and on the hillside to the west is the old Border Tower of Kirkhope, in good order. In 1649 there were a number of houses as well. Farther up the valley is the Tushielaw Inn and to the west the ruins of Tushielaw Tower on a bare hillside 1,500 feet up. A little above Tushielaw, where the Rankle Burn joins the Ettrick, are the modern mansion and ancient ruins of Thirlestane.

There is a bridle-path from the Ettrick to the Yarrow; starting at Wardlaw it finishes at Tibbie Shiels Inn on St. Mary's Loch. James Hogg, the Ettrick Shepherd, spent many a good night at Tibbie Shiels. His remains are in the churchyard of the Church of the Manse of Ettrick along with those of Tibbie herself and others of Scott's friends and characters. St. Mary's Loch is the largest in the south of Scotland and from any of the surrounding hills makes a breathtaking picture. On the narrow neck of land between St. Mary's Loch and the Loch of Lowes is a statue of the Ettrick Shepherd with the last lines of the *Queen's Wake:*

He taught the wandering winds to sing.

Both the Ettrick and the Yarrow are very beautiful valleys with magnificent hills. From Yarrowford a road goes north to Inner-leithen. Newark Castle, on the right-hand side of the Yarrow and looking down on to the road and the river, is a strong and massive tower said to have been built by James II. Although on private land, no objections are raised to the public entrance. This was the scene of the opening portion of the *Lay of the Last Minstrel.* Shortly before reaching Selkirk the heavily wooded hills of the Philiphaugh estate will be seen on the north side of the road. Philiphaugh gives its name to the battle on 13 September, 1645, in which the Royalist leader, the Marquis of Montrose, was defeated by the Roundhead David Leslie.

ABBOTSFORD

SIR WALTER SCOTT'S FAMOUS HOME, Abbotsford, is situated south of Galashiels and just north of Melrose and the Eildon Hills, the lovely haunt of "Thomas the Rhymer" of romantic legend.

The great author bought the land and small farm then known as Carleyhole while he was only just beginning to make his name as a writer, and when he earned his living mainly in the Scottish Law Courts. Scott saw the enormous possibilities of the somewhat neglected, forlorn-looking place: all around it was the countryside of his ancestors, and the view across the Eildon Hills especially was the "country of his heart" always.

Transformation

Sir Walter told Byron that he was "making a silk purse out of a sow's ear" and, having changed the name of the estate, he began slowly, year by year, extending the house, adding rooms, and turning it into a country mansion. Boudoirs were designed, a fine library constructed, and next to it the "study" with a charming little stairway which leads to a gallery some two-thirds of the way up. A large dining-room was created, and all the windows of the best rooms looked out over the sparkling River Tweed.

Ice-cold Burn

By the time the young children of the family had grown up, Abbotsford had been transformed into a good example of "Scots Baronial", and their father had become Sir Walter. In keeping with his romantic nature was the purchase of neighbouring estates, especially Toftfield, the name of which he and his family changed to Huntleyburn. The ice-cold burn clattering over the stones here was the very "Huntlie bank" which Thomas of Ercildoune sat by when he met the enchanting Queen of Elfland and went away with her for seven years. To have Thomas the Rhymer's glen in his own grounds must have delighted the man who so much loved romantic ballads and legends.

Modern Touch

The handsomely panelled hall of Abbotsford contains armour, shields, ancient weapons, and a splendid fireplace. A feature of Scott's hospitality was that a piper from Skye always played for dancing when there were guests. Although the turrets and galleries of the building were in the old tradition, the "Wizard of the North" (as Scott was called), was enterprising enough to light his mansion by gaslight: the first person to do so north of the Border.

A visit to Abbotsford is most rewarding, not only to walk where the great author weaved his magic, but to see his rare and interesting books, collection of unusual weapons, and for a glimpse of the "study" where he wrote so industriously, and successfully, to clear himself from the slur of bankruptcy.

Although visitors may not bring dogs on such a visit, there is a charming little burial-ground of various dogs of the Scott household, set in a quiet corner overlooking the river.

MELROSE

Population: 2,125.
Early Closing Day: Thursday.

M ELROSE STILL RETAINS THE AIR of the narrow streets of the market town of long ago, and for that reason is the more attractive. Legend has it that St. Cuthbert was one of the monks of the tiny settlement on the promontory now known as Old Melrose. It was a little while after these monks had left for County Durham that David I founded Melrose Abbey in 1136, and still after centuries of destruction and rebuilding, it is possibly the most beautiful Abbey of the many in South Scotland. The Abbey Garden, just opposite, is a most delightful and lovingly tended garden where a quiet hour can be well spent. The centre of Melrose is marked by the Market Cross, dated 1662, and with the emblems declaring that this was a Burgh of Regality and later a Burgh of Barony.

The Eildons

As with so many other towns it is the outlying districts that have the most interesting sights. The Eildons, three hills south of and very close to Melrose, must be counted among the great attractions of the area. The centre one is the highest, 1,385 feet. In an area where there are virtually no hills, they stand out in glorious outline at sunrise or sunset. Climb to the top of the highest and enjoy one of the finest and most beautiful of views: flat country to the south, Melrose and the Tweed to the north, while westwards are range upon range of hills disappearing in the distance, and east and south-east are the high hills of the Border, the Cheviot Range.

Scott's View

A mile west of Melrose is the village of Darnick, with a very fine tower dating from 1425. It is a private residence but is well worth a glimpse from the road. The village of Gattonside is on the north bank of the Tweed and connected by suspension bridge; it is a most attractive village and little changed over the centuries. Eastwards from Gattonside the road follows the Tweed past the railway viaduct that was a masterpiece in its day, to Scott's View, from the top of Bemersyde Hill. Here there is room for cars, with an indicator showing the direction of features of interest and the most extraordinarily beautiful view of the Tweed Valley. This was Scott's favourite view.

Dryburgh Abbey

A little farther along the same road is the estate of Bemersyde that was held by the Haig family for centuries. At the end of the 1914—18 war the house and grounds were purchased by public subscriptions and presented to Field-Marshal Earl Haig. Below the tiny village of Dryburgh, with the huge statue of Wallace, is Dryburgh Abbey, in one of the most supremely beautiful and heavily wooded loops of this lovely River Tweed. In 1150 Dryburgh was founded, and through the centuries suffered more heavily even than Melrose. A visit to Dryburgh should be made if only on account of its superb situation.

Smailholm

Across the river are the two largely industrial towns of St. Boswells and Newton St. Boswells. Two miles east and right alongside the Tweed is the outstanding Pele Tower of Smailholm, about which Scott wrote:

> And still I thought the shattered tower
> The mightiest work of human power:
> And marvelled as the aged hind
> With some strange tale bewitched my mind.

KELSO

Population: 5,000.
Early Closing Day: Wednesday.
Tourist Information Office: 66, Woodmarket.

THE BEST THING ABOUT KELSO is the mixture of old and new, Completely new buildings are like friendly neighbours to Georgian houses. The great Square is an outstanding example. Kelso has been designated a town of exceptional architectural value and particularly the Square.

Floors Castle

Long before Kelso came into being there was a Royal Burgh across the River Tweed, Roxburgh; of this ancient town there is nothing left apart from some very slight remains of Roxburgh Castle. The view from the far end of the bridge of Floors Castle, built in 1718 and supposed to have been designed by Sir John Vanbrugh, takes in the junction of the Teviot Water and the Tweed as well as the area of old Roxburgh. There are some lovely riverside walks. The fine, handsome bridge was built by Rennie in 1800.

The Abbey

Kelso Abbey was founded in 1128 and has suffered badly at the hands of the English as well as the later Scottish Reformers. The west end of this great church is about all that is left, and it was at one time one of the largest and richest Abbeys in Scotland.

Springwood Park, on the other side of the river, is the home of the Agricultural Show, Pony and Ram sales. Today Kelso is an agricultural town, its population engaged in servicing and supplying the rich surrounding farming areas.

From many points near the town the views of the Border hills, only seven or eight miles away, are magnificent, and will call to the walker. Along the feet of these hills little valleys run into them, enabling the motorist to explore away from the busy main roads. Morebattle and Town Yetholm, with its close neighbour Kirk Yetholm, are good centres. Kirk Yetholm is the start of the great Pennine Way walk. Just past the village of Ancrum on the A68 and four miles before entering Jedburgh, turn left on the B6400 for the Peniel Heugh Monument to the Battle of Waterloo; it stands on a hill 777 feet up, is over 200 feet in height, and can be ascended by the public. Ancrum is itself a battlefield, the battle of Ancrum having been fought in 1545 between the Scots and Henry VIII of England.

JEDBURGH

Population: 4,000.
Early Closing Day: Thursday.

SITUATED ON THE JED WATER, which starts life on Carter Bar, Jedburgh is the only Royal Burgh in Roxburghshire.

The country around is not spectacular but extremely pleasant, with rolling hills and good farmland. Many lovely runs can be taken from Jedburgh as a centre. Two of the best, southwards, are along the Teviot Water to Hawick and Langholm, or to Bonchester Bridge, Newcastleton and Gretna Green.

Splendid Ruin

In the town itself there are a number of things that should be seen. The Abbey, very much ruined but still a place of splendid grandeur, was founded in 1118. The castle is known to have existed in 1174; it was, however, destroyed in 1409 and replaced in 1823 by the present building, once the prison, which is well worth a visit. Mary Queen of Scots House is the finest monument, apart from the Abbey, and is a treasure house of relics. The house itself is of the greatest interest and the gardens are entirely beautiful. Mary Queen of Scots occupied this house for some considerable time. The Auld Brig, Well House and Richmond Row may be the oldest parts of the town; certainly the bridge has been scheduled as a monument of national importance.

Ferniehirst Castle

One mile south of Jedburgh on the A68 at Hundalee Mill is a massive old Capon tree which is believed to be the last survivor of the medieval Jed Forest. Although its age is obviously not certain it is probably a thousand years old and has had to be supported. A little farther south is Ferniehirst Castle, on the banks of the Jed Water. Its age is unknown but it was partially destroyed in 1571 and shortly afterwards rebuilt. It is now a Youth Hostel. It is typically Scottish and of the greatest interest.

Jedburgh, Auld Brig

HAWICK

Population: 16,500.
Early Closing Day: Tuesday.
Tourist Information Office: Volunteer Park.

ALTHOUGH HAWICK IS LARGELY an industrial town famed all over the world for its tweeds and woollen fabrics, yet it has a number of things to show the visitor. It seems probable that Hawick came into existence somewhere about the eighth or ninth century and in spite of the many centuries of border warfare and internal strife has kept growing since.

There was a tower or castle of Hawick built by the Normans, but all that remains is the Moat, an earthwork about 50 feet high. For many centuries the Douglases were the masters, being replaced in 1675 by the Buccleughs. The Town Hall, or Town House, is a very Scottish building and probably dates from the late seventeenth or early eighteenth century.

Rubers Law

Close to Hawick there are a number of interesting spots. The Hornshole Bridge, the scene of a foray in 1514, the Goldielands Tower close to the Teviot Water, Cavers Village Church, and Wilton Lodge Park with a very fine museum. St. Mary's Kirk in Kirkstile was first dedicated by the Bishop of Caithness in 1214; it has been rebuilt several times, most recently in 1763. The Tower Hotel incorporates a tower dating from the twelfth century. There are many old Border Towers in this district: the Black Tower of the sixteenth century is incorporated in Drumlanrig, Branxholm Castle on the Teviot Water south of Hawick, Allan Haugh Tower and Hollows Tower, one belonging to the Armstrong Clan. Four miles east of the town is Rubers Law, 1,392 feet high and affording some fine views. For the explorer there are many other interesting places.

Hermitage Castle

From Hawick there are some fine motor runs. West through Roberton, Aylemoor Loch, the Ettrick Water and St. Mary's Loch. Follow the Teviot Water south-west through Teviot Head to Langholm, south-east to Bonchester Bridge, then south to Liddelsdale and the famous and infamous Hermitage Castle on the beautiful Hermitage Water, then on to Newcastleton and the south. Or due south to Stobs Castle and Newcastleton. All the above are lovely runs through varied country. The Liddelsdale and Hermitage Castle are particularly associated with the famous Armstrong Clan who, living close to the

English, were always raiding the North Tyne valley, and of course the Robsons and other North Tyne families returned the compliment, so that this part of the border was one of the most warlike.

The Armstrongs
Langholm, to many the bonniest little town in Southern Scotland, is often called the Muckle Toon o' Langholm, muckle meaning strong or brawny, (muckle means great or much in Scotland, but here it has this special meaning) is situated on the River Esk and is in every way worth a visit. It has been said that the Armstrongs, the Liddelsdale clan of long ago, were banished from Langholm and their descendants were sentenced to be hung if they ever returned. Apparently Neil Armstrong, the American astronaut who landed on the Moon for the first time on 20 July 1969 is one of this ancient clan, but Langholm have invited him to return without fear of being hung. It is said that here rugby football was introduced to Scotland. The finest journey back into England, if you have the time, is through Newcastleton, Sautree and cross the border at Deadwater, then follow the North Tyne to Hexham. North-west from Langholm up the River Esk is a particularly fine scenic run.

ANNAN
Population: 6,100.
Early Closing Day: Wednesday.
Market Days: Thursday, Friday.

THE MODERN TOWN OF ANNAN has some of the oldest historical associations. Robert Bruce was Lord of Annandale in the twelfth century. Since those days Annan has suffered and revived, as have all other Border towns. In the last century the port of Annan was known all over the world and a considerable amount of shipbuilding was done. In the Queensberry Arms Hotel is a picture of the famous clipper ship *Queensberry*, the last to be built at Annan. Today this is a market town in a rich agricultural district with a number of industries.

From the river a fine panorama of woodlands extends northwards, while from the higher points the Solway can be seen with the high peaks of Cumberland in the English Lake District.

The Brus Stone
The most outstanding building is the Town House in the Scottish baronial style. The Mote and the nearby museum are among the most ancient. The Brus Stone stands in the courtroom of the Town House

and probably came from the nearby Castle—the date 1300 appears on the stone. A statue to Edward Irving stands in the grounds of Annan Old Church. The Solway Viaduct from Annan to Bowness carried a single railway-track and was considered one of the greatest engineering feats of that day. It has been taken down but the site and the view across which the viaduct spanned is worth seeing.

From Annan there are some glorious runs northwards to the Ettrick Forest and the Lowther Hills, but take the side roads. Gretna Green is eight miles to the east.

GRETNA GREEN

This little village in Dumfries, just over the western border with England was long famous as the haven of runaway lovers who could take advantage there of the old Scots Law (always different from English law despite the Act of Union), and marry instantly without family consent.

The most famous site for these marriages by declaration, which had to be made in the presence only of some suitable sober or established person of the village, was the Blacksmith's Shop, probably because it

was the first placed reached by fugitives. When time and distance was of the essence, minutes might make the difference between success and failure for the runaways. This was the origin of the "marriage over the anvil", although any other shop or cottage would do provided the local people were present to witness the "declaration".

Today Scots law requires a residential qualification of at least twenty-five days and Gretna Green is out of business. However the ghost of old romances and adventures clings to the name and the place while visitors are invited to view "The original Smithy" site, and the later Blacksmith's Shop, and all sorts of mementoes of the past may be purchased by those who are interested.

Of course, eloping couples still flee to Scotland, but they have to fulfil the residential rule, before they can be officially married.

Index

Another superb title in the Geographia range . . .

A Geographia Guide

Northern Scotland
including Orkneys
Shetlands & Hebrides

**your companion and guide
to the Scottish Highlands**